GOSPEL
THE BOOK OF
MARK

A NEW TRANSLATION WITH COMMENTARY—
JESUS SPIRITUALITY FOR EVERYONE

GOSPEL
THE BOOK OF
MARK

THOMAS MOORE

Walking Together, Finding the Way®
SKYLIGHT PATHS®
PUBLISHING
Nashville, Tennessee

SkyLight Paths Publishing
an imprint of Turner Publishing Company
Nashville, Tennessee
New York, New York
www.skylightpaths.com
www.turnerpublishing.com

Gospel—The Book of Mark:
A New Translation with Commentary—Jesus Spirituality for Everyone

2017 Hardcover, First Printing
© 2017 by Thomas Moore

For information regarding permission to reprint material from this book, please write or fax your request to Turner Publishing, Permissions Department, at 4507 Charlotte Avenue, Suite 100, Nashville, Tennessee 37209, (615) 255-2665, fax (615) 255-5081, or email your request to submissions@turnerpublishing.com.

Library of Congress Cataloging-in-Publication Data
Names: Moore, Thomas, 1940- translator, commentator.
Title: The book of Mark : a new translation with commentary : Jesus
  spirituality for everyone / Thomas Moore.
Other titles: Bible. Mark. English. Moore.
Description: Nashville : Turner Publishing Company, 2017. | Series: Gospel |
  Includes bibliographical references.
Identifiers: LCCN 2016052462 | ISBN 9781594736308 (hardcover : alk. paper)
Subjects: LCSH: Bible. Mark--Commentaries.
Classification: LCC BS2583 .M66 2017 | DDC 226.3/05209--dc23
LC record available at https://lccn.loc.gov/2016052462

10 9 8 7 6 5 4 3 2 1

Manufactured in the United States of America
Cover Design: Jenny Buono
Interior Design: Tim Holtz

To Ajeet

Contents

Introduction to Gospel

Why a New Translation?

In my travels I have met many people who grew up hearing the Gospels in church and have now moved on in a different direction. Some have found their religion outmoded or just do not feel like participating any longer. Some have been offended, like many women who find formal religion sexist. Others are attracted to altogether different traditions, and some do not see the point of religion at all.

Many told me they missed the stories and the teachings, and wished they could have a better, more up-to-date understanding of them. I have heard from other people who did not have a Christian background and wondered if the Gospels could enhance their more open-ended spiritual path. I have strong empathy for both positions and wanted to present the Gospels in a way that would speak to both.

Some Christians, both traditional and independent, expressed their fervent curiosity about how I might understand the teachings, given my unusual background as a monk, a student of world religions, and a depth psychotherapist. I felt their eagerness and sincerity when they asked me to recommend a good translation. I could not direct them without reservation to any translation that I knew and trusted, so the idea of my own version took root.

Another reason I felt it was time for a new version was my frustration at seeing faulty religious ideas, specifically about the teachings of Jesus, dragging down important political advances in our society. You do not have to look far beneath the headlines to see uninformed, emotional, and sentimental notions of Jesus's philosophy. Today we cannot afford to keep referring to outmoded and faulty versions of Jesus's teachings and using them to support questionable causes.

In the end, I wanted to make the Gospels accessible and attractive to all sorts of readers. I see no indication that Jesus intended to create a religion or a church. His purpose is clear: He wanted to raise human awareness and behavior to a higher level, where it would surpass its tendencies toward self-interest, xenophobia, greed, religious moralism, and an emphasis on insignificant rules. He imagined a more just and pleasurable world, a "kingdom of the sky." He was explicit in instructing his students to speak to everyone, not just some particular and chosen religious group.

In my translation there is no suggestion that readers should believe in anything, join an organization, or abandon their cherished religious and philosophical ideals. I see no reason why a Christian, an agnostic, a Buddhist, or even an atheist would not be charmed and inspired by the Gospels. Anyone can freely and without any worries read the Gospels and be enriched by them.

These texts are sacred not because they belong to a particular religion or spiritual tradition but because they offer a vision and a way of life that transcends the limits of reason and will. They show a figure in love with life and with a heart open to all sorts of people, but at the same time a figure constantly in tune with the Sky Father, that image of ultimate transcendence that provides an opening, a tear in the fabric of human consciousness, a doorway to the infinite and the eternal.

The Gospels are not just books of practical wisdom—how to live more effectively. They are also books of mysteries, assuming that to be fully human we have to open ourselves to the mysterious depth and height of the world that is our home.

Who Was Jesus?

It is a simple question, isn't it? Who was Jesus? But the debate over the historical Jesus has been raging for at least two centuries. There is not much factual material to go on, and though the Gospels often sound like biography or history, clearly they are largely stories told to evoke a religious milieu. Historically, they are full of contradictions and gaps and fantasy material. This does not make them inherently worthless. On the contrary, they are marvelous, simply ingenious inventions for spiritual teaching. But as history they are unreliable, to say the least.

It appears that Jesus was born around 4 BCE, when Romans were occupying the Mediterranean region of Jesus's birth and travels. Herod the Great was king, having been installed by the Romans. Greek language and culture were strong in the area, and Egypt, with its colorful past and rich spiritual culture, was not far away. There is evidence of a temple to the Greek god Dionysus in Jesus's area, and yet he was also dealing daily with Jewish teachings, customs, and rules. The Gospels portray many verbal skirmishes between Jesus and leaders, religious and social, who spoke up for Jewish law and tradition.

Jesus taught in the synagogues and to some appeared to be the long-awaited Messiah, the anointed leader of a new Jewish order. Many events and sayings in the Gospels echo Hebrew Bible writings, suggesting a layer of Messiah in Jesus's words and actions. But this aspect also casts a shadow on Jesus's presence and work, leading to the notion that he was "king of the Jews" and therefore a threat to Roman, local, and religious authority. Jesus was executed somewhere around 30 CE, perhaps in his early thirties.

It is often said that people who read the Gospels see the Jesus they want to see. Some view him as a religious reformer, others as a social rebel, and still others as the founder of a religious tradition. He is sometimes described as a teacher of wisdom, a label that comes close to my own view but is not quite serious enough. I see him more as a social mystic, like a shaman who can heal and lead people to appreciate multiple layers of their reality.

At his baptism, the sky opens and the Sky Father speaks favorably of him, blessing him. For me, this is a key moment, because Jesus is forever talking about his Father in the Sky, calling on us to live in relation to that transcendent realm, as well as in the present moment, where our goodwill and powers of healing are always needed.

Jesus also has a relationship with the dead, and his own death is always looming. So in the end we have a Jesus who, as shaman and mystic, speaks and acts from the plane of daily life, from the transcendent level of the Father, and in the realm of the dead. He is offering more than lessons in practical wisdom. He offers a profound mystical vision that combines social action, based on the principle of friendship and not just altruism, and an all-embracing mystical awareness of timeless realities and sensibilities.

Some think that Jesus wanted to create a religion or a church. Others note that he was often speaking about the afterlife. In my translation and commentary, I move in a different direction. I think he was trying to convince people to live in an entirely different way, guided by basic values of love and community, instead of self-interest and conflict. He suggested keeping the highest ideals in mind, rather than merely trying to amass money and possessions. He spoke and acted contrary to moralistic laws and customs and showed in his manner of living that friends and good company were worth more than pious activities. He told all his students to be healers and to help people rid themselves of compulsive behaviors. Above all, he suggested that we get over all the artificial boundaries set up between religions and cultures and live as though we were all brothers and sisters. "Who is my family?" he asks (Matthew 12:48), and he points to the students and others gathered around him.

What Is a Gospel?

The story of Jesus's life and teachings was written down, after a fairly long period of oral storytelling, by many writers, each having a different purpose. We get the basics of the story in Mark, strong references to Jewish tradition in Matthew, important elaboration of the stories and teachings in Luke, and a mystical dimension in John. By the fifth century CE, the church had made these four versions official. They are called "canonical," the only ones approved by the church at that time: Matthew, Mark, Luke, and John. These writings first appeared somewhere between 65 CE and 110 CE, at least thirty-five years after Jesus's death. The Book of Mark is the oldest, and the writers of Matthew and Luke took some material from Mark.

So think about that: A teacher appears and dies, and decades later a few devotees write down some stories about his life and try to capture his teachings, based on what had been passed down by word of mouth. Besides problems with memory, the various stories, as we see in the canonical Gospels, each conveyed their own sense of what Jesus was all about. They were interpretations, not histories.

Two millennia later, modern people try to make sense of these written documents. Not being historians, they tend to view the stories as factual and even try to live by their interpretations. Some of the tales are quite fantastic: miraculous healings, raising the dead to life, the teacher himself surviving death, miraculous meals, and angels appearing here and there. Put together these two aspects—fantastic events and a tendency to take every word literally—and you have problems in understanding.

Strictly speaking, the word "Gospel" in the original Greek means "good message." It has been translated as "good news" or "glad tidings," both accurate and beautiful phrases. But what is the good news? That is not so easy to sort out.

The Translation

If you have grown up reading the Gospels or hearing them read in church, you may think that the translation you take for granted is official or sacred. But the Gospels were originally written in a form of Greek spoken by people in everyday life. Historians generally agree that Jesus spoke Aramaic and that the Gospels were written in Greek. There is no widely accepted ancient Aramaic version, though some think that the Greek Gospels, in particular Matthew and Luke, may have been based on Aramaic sources.

If you were to read the Gospels in the original Greek, you would be surprised, maybe even shocked, to see how simple the language is. The vocabulary is limited, and many sentences read almost like a book meant for children. The Book of Luke is somewhat more sophisticated than Mark, and Matthew lies somewhere in the middle. But still the Greek is quite plain. This means that a translator has great liberty in using a number of different words for the simple ones that keep coming up and is likely to infuse his version with his own biases and points of view.

In rendering the Greek Gospels into English, I would like to have come up with astonishing, florid, and entrancing phrases. But, as I said, the original is so simple that it would be a travesty to make a translation too elaborate. I kept two principles in mind as I made this translation: I wanted to give the reader a version that would flow gracefully and be as clear and limpid as I could make it, and I wanted to use striking new English words for a few key terms that I thought were usually misunderstood.[1] I worked hard to be sure that my versions of these words had the backing of history and scholarship.

Jesus as Poet

I see Jesus as a spiritual poet. There is a striking passage in the Book of Matthew where Jesus's students are being literal and he corrects them. Matthew comments, "He said nothing to the people that was not a parable" (Matthew 13:34). By "poet" I do not mean that Jesus speaks or writes poetry, but that he uses narrative, metaphor, and imagery to get his rich ideas across. He does not speak like an academic or a theologian, defining his terms and setting out his ideas pedantically. He is part teacher and part entertainer, a spiritual leader and a bard, a shaman and an enchanter.

A spiritual poet uses language for its beauty and for the power of its imagery. He wants to give the listener or reader insight into life. A poet does not force an understanding of life or an ideology onto his listeners. His narratives and images are meant to deepen a person's view of life. Some topics get lost in highly rationalistic language, while a more imagistic approach better conveys the mysteries involved.

If Jesus says that he speaks in parables, we should have a good idea about what a parable is. People often think of a parable as a simple, moral teaching story. But scripture scholar Robert Funk says that a parable helps us "cross over" into the mysterious land that Jesus is trying to evoke for us, a kingdom in which life is radically different. Similarly, the renowned scholar John Dominic Crossan says that a parable "shatters our complacency" and pulls us out of the comfortable picture of life we have always lived by.

A parable is the opposite of a gentle teaching story. It confronts us, asking us to change our way of seeing things. It turns conventional ideas upside down. Its very point is to make us uncomfortable. In plain teaching in the Book of Matthew, Jesus says, "Love your enemies and speak well of those who criticize you. This way you can become sons of your Father in the Sky. For he makes the sun rise on the bad and the good and rain on the just and the unjust" (Matthew 5:44–45).

For many, this teaching is just too radical. How many people show any love for those they consider enemies? Later Jesus tells the parable of a woman who hid a small amount of yeast in a large pile of flour. That is what the Jesus kingdom is like. It is not overt, not even visible, and its initial effects are tiny. Yet it can change a life and alter the course of the world. If only a small portion of people in the world understood that somehow you have to love your enemies, we might not go on dividing ourselves into the good and the bad, and the Jesus vision would gain some traction.

Much of what is written in the Gospels is poetic in style, sometimes metaphorical and allegorical. You have to have a sharp and sophisticated appreciation for symbol and image or you might completely misread the text.

For example, Jesus heals a blind man. Is this a simple miraculous good deed or does it speak to a less literal blindness? Do we all fail to see life for what it is and have the wrong view of our place in the world? The Gospel writer himself speaks about this more poetic kind of blindness.

A Better Word for "Sin"

Many translations of the Gospels have a moralistic air. The translator may think of Christianity as a religion of do's and don'ts, and that point of view leads him to translate certain words with a heavy moral slant. Take the word "sin," so often used in English versions. Many readers of the Gospels know that the word originally meant "an action that falls shy of the mark." Yet we do not use the word "sin" that way. We mean that someone has done something so bad that it merits everlasting punishment.

As a child growing up in a devout Catholic family, I was always being told, "Don't do that. You'll go to hell." What if an adult had said to me, "There you go again. You're off the mark. You need to get your values straight." At least I would have had a chance to do better.

I do not translate the Greek word *hamartia* as "sin" or even "off the mark." I prefer the reflections of the pre-Christian philosopher Aristotle, who in his book on poetry and drama, *Poetics*, discusses the role of *hamartia* in tragedy. He says it refers to an action done out of ignorance that has tragic consequences.

When I was a child, I had a BB gun and shot some birds. I still feel remorse for doing such a thing. I needed to be taught the value of innocent animal life. My ignorance led me to actions I now regret. I would not say that I committed a sin, but that in my ignorance I made a mistake that today I mourn. I do not consider myself a horrible person and carry that guilt with me, but I understand that I have to keep learning and become more aware so I do not make worse mistakes.

With Aristotle's thoughtful explanation in mind, how would you translate *hamartia*? It is complicated. Maybe several words would be better than one. I tend to use the word "mistake," but I know that alone it sounds too weak. Usually I qualify it according to the context in which it is used. I do not want to imply that *hamartia* is a simple, everyday misstep, but neither do I want to suggest high-minded moralistic judgment, which I do not pick up from the Gospels in Greek. So I often used the phrase "tragic mistake."

I have seen many English translations of the Gospels that try to make the language more modern in style than the familiar, often archaic renditions. I appreciate many of these modern versions, but none interprets the Gospels the way I do. I have my own idea of what the Gospels are about, and my translation expresses that viewpoint. "Sin" is only one of many key words that affect the way we understand what Jesus was up to and what he taught. Not finding "sin" in this translation, I hope you read the Gospels without beating yourself up for having done wrong. I hope you see that Jesus was not moralistic but rather deeply concerned about the roots of self-serving and destructive behavior.

Some Key Images

For years, in writing many books, I have turned to Greek classical literature for insight, especially the great tragedies and comedies, the hymns to the gods and goddesses, and the mythological stories. In the Gospel translation, whenever I come across any connection between the Gospels and these classical sources I take note of the crossover and see if it offers any special insight. In some cases, the parallels are striking and in others subtle and hidden. In general, an awareness of earlier uses of Greek terms helps us understand better what is being said in the Gospels.

As a student of both religion and depth psychology, I have spent many years studying Greek polytheism. I have been amazed by the richness, complexity, and insightfulness of the ancient tales of the gods and goddesses. If you were to read some of the penetrating essays by my mentor, the psychologist James Hillman, or the well-known mythologist Joseph Campbell, you would see how the old Greek stories help us gain insight into the patterns and dynamics of our everyday lives.

As I was poring over the Greek text of the Gospels, studying one key word or phrase after another, I discovered several instances in which a reference to one of the ancient Greek stories lay buried in the etymology or structure of the word itself.

The Kingdom of the Sky

The clearest example is the phrase "kingdom of heaven" or "our Father who art in heaven." The Greek word usually translated as "heaven" is *ouranos.* The word could be taken as an ordinary term for the sky, but it is also the name for the sky-god of the Greeks, Ouranos, today usually spelled "Uranus," like the planet.

When I read the words "kingdom of heaven" (*ouranos*), I am inclined to translate the phrase as "kingdom of the sky." I will say more about this image later, but my point here is that the Greek version of the Gospels has layers and, whether intentional or not, deep themes peek through and enrich the stories and teachings.

The Kingdom

You get the sense in the Gospels that Jesus is an intimate and special son of the Sky Father. The kingdom he is creating on earth is a way of life sanctioned by this Father. When asked how to pray, Jesus says, "Say, 'Our Father in the Sky, may your name be held sacred....'"

I see the sky as a metaphor or, better yet, an archetypal image. Its meaning is based on ordinary experience: You look at the sky at night, or even during the day, and you may wonder about the meaning of everything and your place in life. You may imagine other worlds, other planets, and other civilizations. You may look into the light-blue daytime heavens or the blue-black night sky and sense infinity and eternity. The kingdom of the sky, therefore, is not akin to practical, factual, and self-absorbed life. It is an alternative, the object of wonder and perfection, eternal and infinite. The "Father" of that realm offers a more perfected idea of what human life could be.

The kingdom of the sky comprises those people who live the values Jesus specifies in his teaching, especially the one about respecting any person who is not of your circle. Jesus does not talk about love as a sentimental emotion. That is why I usually translate *agape* as "respect." If your basic motivation in all of life is love and respect, you are automatically in the kingdom. But take note: Jesus makes it clear that your actions have to follow your values in this regard.

The Sky and the Sky Father

I prefer to use the word "sky" instead of "heaven" because it is a concrete image. I do not mean a literal father in the clouds but rather the sky as an image for spirit. As I have read the passages about the Sky Father, I have had in mind the Native American mystic Black Elk, praying to the parents and grandparents in the sky.

Here is a typical passage from Black Elk that influenced me in translating *Ouranos*:

> The fifth Grandfather spoke, the oldest of them all, the Spirit of the Sky. "My boy," he said, "I have sent for you and you have come. My power you shall see!" He stretched his arms and turned into a spotted eagle hovering. "Behold," he said, "all the wings of the air shall come to you, and they and the winds and the stars shall be like relatives. You shall go across the earth with my power." Then the eagle soared above my head and fluttered there; and suddenly the sky was full of friendly wings all coming toward me.[2]

This passage has much in common with the Gospels, as when Jesus is baptized and the Father speaks from the sky and the spirit appears as a hovering dove. The Gospel describes the sky as sometimes full of not wings, but angels—close.

Hesiod, one of the early Greek spiritual poets, describes *Ouranos*—the word used every time for Gospel phrases like "kingdom of the sky" and "our Father in the heavens"—this way:

> *The first one born of Gaia (Earth) was Ouranos.*
> *He was as big as she was.*
> *He was the sky full of stars.*
> *He spread over her*
> *and was*
> *a solid ground for the holy immortals.*

You can pray to the Father, as Jesus did, and yet know that you are addressing something mysterious and vastly spiritual. Our usual anthropomorphic—humanlike—language is only an approximation of the sublime mystery of this Father. As the spirit of the sky, he is the "ground for the holy immortals" or, we might say, "the ground for our spiritual vision."

The kingdom of the sky, or the heavens, is a place set apart because of its special values and the primacy of its rule of love and respect, *agape*. Jesus wants neither the rule-bound religion of the church officials nor the self-satisfied realm of the purely secular. He calls for a third alternative, a place where you can live a life based on spiritual values of love and respect.

The Commentary

Because the concepts in the Gospels are so nuanced, I have included many notes on the translation and comments on the meaning. Some of them come from other sources, offering either an expert reflection on the passage or special insight from an artist. From the beginning I wanted to include comments from thinkers of many different spiritual traditions. Why not? Their different perspectives open up fresh ways of understanding the Gospel stories and teachings. I try to set aside my own academic interests and get to the heart of the matter. If I mention an expert or a writer from history, like Aristotle's thoughts about mistakes or a poet like Anne Sexton, I do not call on them as authorities, as though I were writing a school paper. I mention them because their brilliant ideas are relevant. I hope that their way of seeing the issue will enrich your reading of the Gospels.

Most of the time my comments are my own take on the passage in question. A friend advised me on this project as follows. "People aren't going to read your version because you're a scholar or have a mind-blowing translation to offer. They'll want to know what you think about the various stories and teachings. They want to know your ideas because you write about the soul and how to live more deeply and with less conflict." I heard what he said and beefed up my own commentary in response.

I want to open up the Gospel message by showing how people of various traditions and expertise interpreted certain passages. I quote Christian, Jewish, Sufi, Buddhist, and secular writers; poets, politicians, theologians, and Bible experts. Then I bring my own point of view to various passages, basing my reflections on my studies in depth psychology, world religions, mythology, and the arts. I rely on decades of experience as a psychotherapist, and I am aware of my own development in relation to the Gospels, from my childhood, when I heard them naively; to my monastic days, when I studied them in a Christian context; to now, when I blend the sacred and secular in everything I do and when I am always the psychotherapist. I could make a case that Jesus was a psychotherapist, and, in fact, the word "therapy" is often used in the Greek version to denote Jesus as a healer.

I think that the deeper point of the Gospels has been lost over the years, when people have focused on them as a source of strict moral lessons and the cornerstones for belief, and as the bedrock for the establishment of a religion, church, or spiritual community. To me, Jesus says clearly that he is speaking to everyone who will listen, and his message is suffused with sophisticated psychological insight. My intention with the commentary is to release the Gospels from their narrow confinements and show how valuable they are today to anyone looking for insight into how to live deeply and lovingly.

The Gospels Are for Everyone

Returning to a close study of the Gospels has helped me personally with my spiritual life. These texts now inspire me more forcefully than at any time in my life. I do not see them as representing or advocating for a particular religious viewpoint but as pointing to a way of life, a secular set of values, that could help humanity survive and thrive. While I certainly do not want to convert anyone to a particular religion or church, I would like to see the whole world adopt this vision for humanity, based on love, respect, healing, and compassion.

I hope this new translation will move us in a more thoughtful, subtle, and compassionate direction in our own way of living and in our attitude toward others, especially those different from us. This is a key part of Jesus's teachings: He is forever telling people to love those who are outside their own circle. The kingdom is for them, he says, not for the in crowd.

My own practice is to keep at hand several different translations of sacred texts. I have seven versions of the Tao Te Ching on my shelves, close at hand. I recommend doing the same with the Gospels. For example, I have relied on the beautiful translation by Robert W. Funk and the Jesus Seminar in a book called *The Acts of Jesus*. I respect the scholarship behind that translation, though I did not want to use such complicated language in my own version. I admire the witty and profound translations of certain passages by John Dominic Crossan in his book *The Essential Jesus*. "The somebodies will be nobodies and the nobodies will be somebodies." You cannot get a better translation than that.

If you are looking for a more extravagant version or something completely different, those translations are available. But if you want an accurate version that is close to the original in vocabulary and tone, presented in simple, rhythmic English, then mine might do. If you want help understanding the sometimes difficult passages, not from a scholar's point of view but from someone with a background in depth psychology, literature, and world religions, then you may want to add this one to your collection.

It is my conviction that the less literally you take most passages, the more you will be inspired to live an altogether different kind of life, one in which your heart is more open than you ever thought it could be. You will have found a kind of utopia, an island of meaning radically different from the one that governs the world today. You can live this way now and find joy and substance in your life. And you can promote it as a way for the future—not a belief system or a church or religion, but a way of being in the world, open and radically accepting.

Introduction to the Book of Mark

The Book of Mark is the oldest of the Gospels, written in 65 CE or perhaps a few years later. It is also the shortest of the Gospels and has often received less attention and respect, compared to the other Gospels.

But the Book of Mark is fascinating in its own right, if for no other reason than it is full of mysterious stories and a willingness to not sew things up into tidy conclusions. The ending, for example, leaves the resurrection unreported and offers a strange tone of incompletion and even failure: "Shaken and confused, the women left and hurried away from the tomb. They didn't say a word to anyone, they were so afraid."

This conclusion sounds like Samuel Beckett's *Waiting for Godot*—nothing happens. Quiet and stillness. Fear rather than courage. Empty rather than full. Wonder rather than hope.

The ending also helps us leave open our minds and imaginations to the implications of Jesus's purpose and his proposal of a new way of being. Throughout history, one person after another has appeared to tell us what Christianity is and how we should think and behave. What if we simply allow readers to be affected by the story Mark tells and learn to be led into wonder, remain full of questions, and gradually discover what the Jesus kingdom is all about—for themselves?

In other words, the various expressions of wonder, amazement, and even fright can be the reader's experience as well. I kept this idea in mind as I translated the Book of Mark. Where I felt astonished and puzzled at the mysterious, uncanny, open-ended, and sometimes fantastic scenes, I conveyed that feeling to the reader, as it echoes the classic description of the Holy by theologian and scholar Rudolf Otto: "*Mysterium tremendum et fascinans*," a mystery both unsettling and fascinating.

Mark uses several different words for "amazement," some of them tinged with fear. We get the sense that something extraordinary is at work as Jesus reveals his power, is demanding of his students, and both attracts and disturbs the people who come out to see and hear him. This is not the ultrasensitive, caring Jesus but one who inspires unsettling wonder.

Jesus is not just a teacher of wisdom, not merely a moral crusader, and not a simple storyteller trying to get across simple lessons on how to live. He is not a self-help workshop leader nor is he promoting a new religion.

Jesus keeps his attention on the sky and the Father he envisions there. He frequently goes off on his own to pray. His kingdom is not just a tweaking of life as we know it, but also a penetrating, radical, utopian vision of how human life could be. His goal seems to be to transform earth.

Miracles and Our Miraculous Life

Miracles play an important role in the Book of Mark, so it might be helpful to reflect on them briefly.

In my youth I was always under the impression that the point of the miracles was to prove that Jesus was not just an ordinary person, but also divine. Now, looking for proof does not seem right to me. It comes from anxiety about being right and about trusting the Jesus story. I also keep in mind Ralph Waldo Emerson's comment on miracles in his divinity school address: "The word Miracle ... gives a false impression; it is Monster. It is not one with the blowing clover and the falling rain."[1] Instead of feeling comfortable with our belief in a figure who can prove his worthiness, we could instead wonder at the beauty and perfection of a world in which clover blows and in which Jesus appears to offer a more complete and fulfilled version of humanity.

Two stories in the Book of Mark are particularly puzzling and important: Jesus walking on water and Jesus asleep on the boat during a raging storm. I prefer not to call these miracles. The first is a fantasy tale and the other a great metaphor. Let me explain.

Walking on Water

The first story:

> It was around the fourth watch of the night and he went out to them walking on the water and almost passed them by. When they saw him walking on the lake they thought he must be a phantasm. They all saw him and were afraid and screamed.
>
> He spoke to them then: "Take heart. It's me. Nothing to fear."

He almost passed them by? What was he doing? Heading to the other side of the lake, that is, the Sea of Galilee, some say. But this odd detail shows the gulf between Jesus at home in another level of reality and the students trying to make sense of him. The Greek word for what they saw is *phantasma*, meaning "apparition" or "phantasm." We can argue all day about an explanation for the phenomenon, but we know that in these stories Jesus can appear in a fantastic form, such as when he is transfigured on a mountain. Jesus seems to be, as he says, both an earth being and a sky being. He is attended by angels and has some intimacy with demons, and at the same time he is a loving, kind, friendly, openhearted human.

Faced with a story like this, you can decide whether you believe in literal sky beings and fantasy figures or not, or you can realize that the genre of this Gospel is clearly not history or theology in the usual meaning of the word. Many people treat the Gospels as instructions on living morally or cementing one's belief. But this Gospel, anyway, uses strong fantasy elements to make the point that we are aiming at utopia here, a way of human life that is not limited by the usual laws and expectations. It is a life that inspires awe and wonder and that is seriously different from ordinary reality.

The Raging Storm

The other lake story:

> A turbulent squall came up and waves swept over the boat and almost swamped it. Jesus was in the back of the boat, sleeping on a cushion. The students woke him up. "Teacher, aren't you worried that we'll drown?"
>
> He got up, hushed the wind and shouted to the waves, "Quiet. Calm down." The wind died down and a great calm descended.
>
> He said to his followers, "Why are you so jittery? Are you still lacking in trust?"
>
> They were terrified and said to each other, "Who is this? The wind and the waves obey him."

You can read this story, too, as proof of Jesus's divine power or as a commentary on our relationship to the natural world. I like to think of the turbulent water as an image for the stormy times in life when we are afraid for our emotional survival. If you embrace the Jesus way and develop a big vision for how life works, you may find the trust needed to relax during life's inevitable storms.

Inspiring the Shift

As I was working on this passage on the raging storm, I received a note from a woman I do not know, telling me that she had been in an automobile accident and had severe brain damage. She has little idea who she was before the accident or who she is now. She is trying to forge a new life and identity.

In the midst of all this confusion and uncertainty, she sounded calm and grounded at the center of herself. She said she is a psychotherapist, and I felt she must be a good one to handle her own tragedy so well. Her story reminded me of Jesus and the stormy lake. She seemed to embody that freedom from anxiety that is a gift of the kingdom of the sky. Like Jesus, she seemed to be resting on a cushion amid the tempest and panic all around her.

Her sense of calm reminded me of why I wanted to devote so much energy and time to translating and exploring the Gospels. Not only could they help us establish world peace and community, but they could also help us individually shift to a new level of understanding and lifestyle, where we can find peace and calm, deep relief from the existential anxiety associated with life in complicated times.

As Jesus says many times, being in the kingdom requires "trust in life." Many translations translate the Greek word for this as "faith." But that can imply dedication to a tradition or litany of beliefs. There is not much heart and soul in that kind of faith. But faith as profound trust, especially when life assaults us, is both rare and life-saving.

Reaching for Utopia

The Book of Mark presents a long struggle between Jesus and his students. They never seem to understand who he is and what he is trying to accomplish. They tend to be literalists and fail to see the deeper strands of meaning in his words and actions. They betray him and do not show up for his trial and execution. They complain when the woman at Bethany rubs oil on his feet, an action that points to the profound mystery of his death and resurrection.

The Greeks use the word *agon* for a contest or struggle like this, not a literal fight over property and possessions but a long give-and-take over meaning. In ancient times the *agon* might be an athletic event, but even games point to a deeper struggle.

Scholars see the roots of this struggle in the Hebrew Bible, and their analyses can be enlightening. But my approach to the Gospels does not dwell on Jewish history and literary prefigurings, as so many studies do. I consider all this work of great importance, and I have consulted it and value it highly. But I would like to appreciate the Gospels in a different way, as speaking to our contemporary *agon*, especially our struggle over the materialistic science and lived philosophy of our times. They address the idea that Jesus envisioned a different, equally sophisticated way of being, aiming at a utopian raising of human sensibility toward a deep-seated, global feeling for community and the emotions and intentions that foster it.

Like most of us, Jesus's students have good intentions, but they cannot keep up with the radical nature of his vision. After intense instruction and example, they still want personal gain, standing, security, and favoritism. One minute they profess their allegiance and the next minute they engage in various forms of betrayal.

I always keep the image of the kingdom at the forefront of my understanding of the Gospels, and here I see how difficult it is to discern and then sign up for a way of life that is so radically different from the norm. I can see how many churches profess to represent Jesus and the Gospels, and yet they operate on the principles of the old life, not the new utopian one. It takes struggle, experiment, renewed vision, and courage to try this new way. It is often presented as easy to take on, but it could be the most difficult thing we do in our lifetime.

THE BOOK OF
MARK

1   The first word of the Book of Mark in the Greek is *arche*, meaning "begin-
    ning." There is no definite article, no "the." Just "beginning." This start of
    the Gospel is similar to John, which begins *en arche*, "in beginning." *Archai* is
    a special power word for the Greeks. It was the focus of the early philoso-
    phers who were looking for the origin of life, not scientifically but spiritually.
    What the Greek mythology scholar Marcel Detienne says about the poet
    applies to the Gospel writer: "The poet's speech strives to discover the ori-
    gins of things, primordial reality."
        —Marcel Detienne, *The Masters of Truth in Archaic Greece*, trans. Janet Lloyd
        (New York: Zone Books, 1996), 41

2   Malachi 3:1.

3   Isaiah 40:3.

4   "The sky itself directly reveals a transcendence, a power, and a holiness....
    The symbolism is an immediate notion of the whole of consciousness, of the
    man, that is, who realizes himself as a man, who recognizes his place in the
    universe."
        —Mircea Eliade, *Patterns in Comparative Religion*, trans. Rosemary Sheed
        (Lincoln: University of Nebraska Press, 1996), 38–39

Chapter 1

The Gospel of Jesus Christos, a son of God: Beginning.[1]
Isaiah the prophet wrote:

> *I send my scout ahead*
> *to prepare your path.*[2]
> *The voice of someone*
> *howling in the desert:*
> *"Prepare the master's way*
> *and clear his path."*[3]

John arrives. He baptizes in the desert and tells of a transforming baptism that absolves people of their ignorance and mistakes. Everyone in the countryside of Judea and all Jerusalem make the trek to see him, and, as they admit their faults, he baptizes them in the Jordan River.

John wore camel's hair clothing and a leather belt and ate locusts and wild honey. His message: "Someone more powerful than I follows me. I'm not worthy enough to bend down and loosen the thongs of his sandals. I baptize you in water. He will baptize you in Holy Spirit."

At that time Jesus left Nazareth and went into Galilee, where John baptized him in the Jordan River. Coming up out of the water, Jesus saw a crack in the sky and a spirit looking like a dove hovering over him. A voice sounded from above:[4] "You are my son. I love you. I am very happy with you."

Without delay, the spirit sent him out into the desert where he stayed for forty days. Satan tempted him and then wild animals and angels soothed him.

5   Flavius Josephus (37 CE–c. 100 CE), a Jewish scholar, says that Herod Anti-
pas, on the urging of his wife, imprisoned John the Baptist in Herod's fortress,
Machaerus, near the Dead Sea. The story is in Matthew 14:1–12.

6   The people are amazed, not just impressed. The Greek word, *ekplesso*, is
a strong one. You are knocked over or struck by something astonishing.
The word can also refer to being seized with panic. Obviously, Jesus's mere
presence and the manner in which he speaks and acts strikes many people
and they wonder how he differs from other teachers they know. If we could
feel some of that awe and wonder, we might better convey the spirit of the
Gospel message and the idea of the kingdom.

7   "Unclean spirit" in the Greek is *pneuma acatharton*; that is, a spirit not sub-
jected to catharsis (a-catharsis). "Spirit" and "catharsis" are two important
words in the Gospels. You do not have to think of "spirit" literally as an invisible creature somewhere in the space around you. It may be a family spirit
or the spirit of joy that might pervade you. But the spirit is not cathartic. It
has not been cleaned up. It works against you and your world. Sometimes a
spirit like this is similar to what some psychologists call a "complex," an urge
that often gets in your way and causes you to do bad things. Therapy can do
the job of catharsis by clearing up the gist of the complex that has a hold on
you. In this way, Jesus is a master therapist.

8   It is as though Jesus does not want the demon to betray him by letting it be
known who Jesus is. This implies that Jesus might have wanted to keep his
identity a secret, or that the Gospel writer did not want to reveal too much.
In any case, the demon may make the person he inhabits sick. He also seems
to be familiar with the realm Jesus comes from. Are the demons and Jesus
similar in some respects, perhaps more—or other—than human? We find
two fascinating forms of expression in Mark: amazement and secrecy. Both
indirectly emphasize the extraordinary power of Jesus and the big question
about what kind of being he is.

After John went to prison,[5] Jesus traveled to Galilee to present the exciting news about the divinity. "The time is ripe," he said. "The kingdom of God is approaching. Change your attitude toward life and put your trust in the gospel."

As Jesus walked along the Sea of Galilee, he saw Simon and his brother Andrew, fishermen, tossing a net into the lake. "Join me and I will show you how to fish for people." Without any delay they left their nets and joined up with him.

He went a bit further and saw James, son of Zebedee, and his brother John fixing nets in a boat. He called to them and they left their father, Zebedee, in the boat with a worker and joined up.

They traveled to Capernaum and he taught in the synagogue on the Sabbath. His teaching amazed the people, because he taught them like someone with authority, not like the law professors.[6]

It was then that a man with an unclean spirit appeared in the synagogue.[7] He shouted out: "Jesus of Nazareth. What are you doing here with us? Are you here to exterminate us? I know who you are: the holy one from God."

Jesus scolded him. "Be quiet. Come out of him."[8] The unclean spirit threw the man into a convulsion and left him with a shriek. They were all shocked and talked it over. "What is this? A new teaching? Real authority? He orders unclean spirits around. They do what he says."

Soon his reputation grew in the area all around Galilee.

9   Drawn from the Greek *egeiren*, which means "lifted up," this passage empha-
    sizes key activities of the Jesus kingdom: waking and rising. *Egerio* means to
    get up, wake up, or resurrect. To be part of the kingdom you have to do all
    three things: (1) wake up from your intellectual and cultural stupor and stu-
    pid self-regard; (2) get up, make your vision known, and do something about
    it; and (3) resurrect yourself by becoming a new kind of person, no longer
    soul-dead.

10 A very mysterious statement. Like a shaman, Jesus is familiar with the realm
    of spirits. He can heal because he does not approach the spiritual in its dark
    aspect, as an ordinary person does, afraid because of how foreign it is. He is
    acquainted with that world and can handle it. You do not want to come as a
    stranger to the dark side of life, but as one who knows it well and can deal
    with it fearlessly.

11 In my translation I move back and forth between "demon" and "the demonic."
    I want to suggest that Jesus exorcises the human tendency to act demoni-
    cally; that is, to show fear of the other by ostracizing and acting prejudicial
    against him or her. In the Gospels, there is a connection between the posi-
    tive ideal of loving your neighbor and being blinded by a demonic fear of
    the other that translates into xenophobia.

12 The Greek word here again is *katharos*, or "catharsis"—clean, neat, or pure.
    The implication is not so much being healed of a disease as having things put
    back in order; perhaps no longer considered tainted by an illness. One of our
    spiritual objectives could be to clean up the messes in our lives. "Catharsis,"
    a word that appears frequently in the Gospel writings, is a good focus for
    healthy spiritual living. You try to keep your mind and your intentions clean,
    not neurotically pure but clear of prejudice and ignorant intolerance, free of
    any violence, and positively open to difference and diversity among people.

13 Here, as in many instances, Jesus supports following the religious laws. It is
    the empty and hypocritical insistence on observance that gives rise to his
    anger.

He left the synagogue and with James and John entered the house of Simon and Andrew, where Simon's mother-in-law was in bed with a fever. They didn't wait to tell him about her, but he went up to her and took her by the hand and helped her up.[9] The fever vanished and she took care of them.

That evening, at sundown, people brought the sick and the demonically possessed to Jesus. The whole city, it seemed, gathered around the door. He tended to many afflicted with various diseases, and expelled any demonic presences. He would not allow the demons to speak, though, because they knew him.[10]

In the morning, when it was still dark, he got up and went out to a deserted place and prayed. Simon and his companions looked for him and when they found him they said, "Everyone is looking for you."

Jesus said, "Let's go to the towns nearby. I want to speak there, too. That's why I've come." So he traveled throughout Galilee, speaking in synagogues and getting rid of the demonic.[11]

A man with skin problems came to him and bowed down and begged him, "If you want to, you could clear this up."

Filled with emotion, Jesus stretched out his hand and touched the man. "I do want to," he said. "Be clean." Immediately the man's lesions left him and his skin cleared up.[12]

Jesus sent him away with a strong warning, "Don't tell anyone about this. Just go and show yourself to the priest and offer the sacrifice that Moses prescribed for your cleansing.[13] Leave a testimony." But the man went and broadcast the news and got the word out. So Jesus couldn't go into the town freely but had to stay in the countryside, where people came to him from all over the area.

1 Considering the sheer radical quality of Jesus's message of love and community, it is surprising that so many people are drawn to his message. The kingdom has not arrived; we do not have a world operating on the principle of mutual respect, but people intuitively aspire to such a world.

2 Scripture scholar Wendy Cotter refers to research on tombs having roofs through which a body might be let down and the idea of friends desperate to help a paralyzed person into the divine presence. She writes:

> In my view, the overlap of these images allowed for a metaphorical interpretation of the story. The state caused by sin is that of the living dead. Thus, the paralyzed man, alive but inert like the dead, was a perfect symbol. As sin deadens the soul so God's forgiveness returns the soul to its full life.
> —Wendy Cotter, *The Christ of the Miracle Stories: Portrait through Encounter* (Grand Rapids: Baker Academic, 2010), 104–105

Eighteenth-century Swedish theologian Emanuel Swedenborg, with even more poetic license, refers to the roof as the celestial realm and the room below as the innermost part of a person.
> —Emanuel Swedenborg, *Arcana Coelestia*, vol. 12 (Chester, PA: Swedenborg Foundation, 1978), 10184

I think of the roof dug open by the friends as a kind of Roman Pantheon, the ceiling open and life and spirit pouring in.

3 Jesus often rewards any special effort made to be healed or just to be near him. It may seem like a small point, but making an extra effort shows real engagement and can be a powerful element in healing and spiritual enlightenment.

Chapter 2

After a few days he returned to Capernaum. People heard that he was home, and a large number gathered, so many that there wasn't enough room for them, not even at the door.[1] He was presenting the teaching, when some people came in, four of them, carrying a person who was paralyzed. They couldn't get him to Jesus, so they cleared out an opening in the roof above Jesus and made their way through it and lowered the mat the man was on.[2]

When Jesus saw their sincerity,[3] he said to the paralyzed man, "Child, the mistakes you've made in life are pardoned." Some of the experts in the law were sitting there wondering in their hearts, "How can this man talk that way? It's blasphemy. Who can pardon wrongdoing except God himself?"

4   When we do something wrong, we need forgiveness just to get back into life clear and unburdened. We may need to forgive ourselves, and we may need to be pardoned by the person or persons we have offended. Jesus shows that the pardon by a special teacher or spiritual representative can also be effective because we need the forgiveness of the Sky Father, an absolute forgiveness that is beyond the personal.

5   Or the Sea of Galilee, which is actually a heart-shaped, freshwater lake.

6   Notice the reference to eating. The Gospels often depict Jesus enjoying dinner with his students, friends, and others. Add to this picture Jesus's many references to food in his stories and teachings, and you get the picture of a very human man who enjoys friendship, lively conversation, and good dining. Together these qualities suggest that Jesus has a strong Epicurean streak in him. This in contrast to many other spiritual teachers, who present themselves as ascetics and usually advocate self-denial over pleasure.

7   The renowned scholar John Dominic Crossan uses a term from anthropology—"commensality"—to explain the emphasis on eating with different sorts of people, including those who are not in your usual circle. This is a key idea in Jesus's teaching and a central characteristic of the kingdom. You go out of your way to welcome into your life those who do not usually sit at your table.

8   This passage reflects in a small way Jesus's Epicurean attitude toward life. There is a time for joy and a time for sadness. Fasting is fine, but not at a time when you want to celebrate life. Jesus's presence signifies the moment of transformation in human culture, a turning point toward the highest values. This joyous occasion is not a time for rituals of penance. His message is not glum, but cheerful.

Jesus instantly sensed that they were discussing these issues and said, "Why are you thinking these things? What would be easier, to say to this sick man, 'You're pardoned' or to say, 'Take up your mat and walk?' I want you to understand that the son of man has the power to pardon wrongdoing."[4] Then he told the man, "Pick up your mat and go home." The man stood up, picked up his mat, and went out in plain view. They were all amazed. "We've never seen anything like this," they said.

Then Jesus went out near the lake.[5] A large group arrived and he instructed them. Then, as he was walking along, he saw Levi, son of Alphaeus, sitting at the revenue booth. "Join me," Jesus said, and Levi got up and followed him.

Jesus had dinner at Levi's place.[6] Several tax officials and unsavory people were sitting with him and his followers and hanging around in large numbers. When some Pharisees and lawyers saw him eating with outcasts and revenue officers, they asked his followers, "Why does he eat with these people?"[7]

Jesus heard this and said, "Healthy people don't need a doctor. But the sick do. I haven't come to wake up people who are doing good but those who are doing wrong."

John's followers and the Pharisees were fasting. So some people came to Jesus and asked, "Why is it that John's followers and the Pharisees' followers are fasting, but yours aren't?"

Jesus answered, "Why would the bridegroom's best friends fast while he is with them? While he's present, it would be wrong to fast. The time will come for him to go away, and then they should fast.[8]

9   Sometimes we are tempted to make improvements on the old ways—the materialistic, unconscious life, the way we have always done things. But this image suggests a new container altogether. That container is the kingdom, a fresh spirituality or philosophy of life sketched out in many ways in the Gospels. We need radical change, not tweaks to the status quo.

10 Jesus is consistent in breaking rules that go against basic human needs. In other words, he is not a legalist or a moralist. This is a key concept in the kingdom: You are moral when you treat people well, but not necessarily when you strictly follow the rules.

11 There is considerable discussion on the meaning of this phrase, "son of man." Most likely it simply refers to a human being. Here is scripture scholar Morton Smith's plain summary of the issue:

> In Hebrew and Aramaic "son of" is commonly used to mean "member of the class of"; hence, "the sons of god" is a regular way of saying "the gods," just as "the sons of men"... is a regular way of saying "men."
> —Morton Smith, *Jesus the Magician* (San Francisco: HarperSanFrancisco, 1978), 101

12 The other issue here is being "master of the Sabbath." For a long time, many people have felt that they are under the rules of religion and rarely on top of them. Jesus seems to propose making your own decisions about how to observe holy times and places.

"No one patches a fabric with a piece of cloth that has not been shrunk. If he does, the patch will pull away and make the hole worse. No one pours fresh wine into old winebags. If he does that, the wine will burst the skins, and the wine and the skins will be ruined. Instead, he pours new wine into new winebags."[9]

Once, on the Sabbath, Jesus was walking through a field of grain with his followers. They picked some of the grain. The Pharisees said to him, "See that? Why are they breaking the law of the Sabbath?"

He responded, "Did you ever read about David and his companions in the days of the high priest Abiathar? They were hungry and tired, so David went into the house of God and ate the holy bread. For anyone other than the priests, this would have been unlawful. But David even gave some to his companions."[10]

Jesus said, "The Sabbath was made for people, not people for the Sabbath. The son of man[11] is master of the Sabbath."[12]

1   This is one of those occasions when Jesus gets angry over the thick-headedness
    of the legalists. The Greek word *poros*, which I translate as "dried out," means
    having passages or pores, like the holes in sponges or bones afflicted with
    osteo*poros*is. Anger is an important emotion, alerting us when we are being
    treated badly. As usual, the figure of Jesus is blessed with a sophisticated
    psychology. He uses his anger well.

2   This, of course, is a common theme throughout the Gospels: The religious
    legalists turn to murderous thoughts, choosing to see a law broken rather
    than suffering allayed. This turn toward evil on the part of the religious
    scholars shows how deep-seated are the emotions behind strict observance
    of religious rules. Generally speaking, these powerful feelings roil below the
    surface, so much so that rarely do we talk about the emotional aspects of
    religious obedience.

    Spiritual leadership can easily turn coarse and tyrannical. We usually
    consider the spiritual as so good and well-intentioned that we overlook its
    capacity to promote authoritarianism and domination. It is the deeper soul
    that makes us human and helps us feel empathy with others. But our spiri-
    tuality can become so removed from our humanity that we inflict emotional
    violence on others without compunction.

Chapter 3

On another occasion, Jesus went into the synagogue and ran into a man with a shrunken hand. Some of those present were looking for an excuse to accuse Jesus, so they observed him closely to see if he would heal on the Sabbath. Jesus said to the man with the disfigured hand, "Stand up so that everyone can see you."

Jesus asked them, "What is lawful on the Sabbath? To do good or evil, to save a life or to kill?"

They kept quiet.

He looked around at them and got angry. Their dried-out hearts upset him, so he said to the man, "Give me your hand."[1]

The man put his hand out and it was completely restored. The Pharisees left and began to think about how they might assassinate Jesus.[2]

3   Touching a person, if only someone you are in love with, is not just an expressive gesture but also one that has special potency. Holding hands is a way of being in touch with the other person's "electricity." It is understandable that people in need of healing want to touch Jesus the healer for the transfer of healing power.

4   This is a mysterious theme that keeps popping up: The evil spirits seem familiar with Jesus. They can communicate with him and they know his secrets. Jesus's presence and his teachings are not just about rational moral issues. Always lurking in the background is a connection to a world behind or above this one, another level of reality. Jesus's frequent references to the sky have their counterpart in his mysterious connection to unclean spirits.

5   Commentators often point to the parallel between "the twelve" among Jesus's followers and the twelve tribes of Israel. But the number twelve has deeper and more universal meaning. Why do we order food and other things in dozens and half dozens? Early Christian writers find many ways to explain key numbers like twelve, which is the product of three times four, spirit and earth, perfection and ordinariness, divine and human, heavenly and worldly. In his *Exposition on the Psalms*, St. Augustine derives the number twelve from the Trinity (three) times the four directions. The early Christian theologian Origen simply sees Jesus's twelve apostles echoing the twelve tribes of Israel.

6   In his famous doctrine of the "divine furors," Plato mentions a religious mania or madness. It is a creative and positive way to be swept away by an idea or project. Artists also know the experience well. The strength of Jesus's personality and the power of his vision apparently lead people to wonder if he is creatively inspired or insane. We, too, can look closely into ourselves to determine if there is neurosis in our spiritual excitement. It is not easy to detect, because we usually so love the object of our fascination. Signs of it are fanaticism, rigidity, literalism, moralism, self-denial, righteous anger, and extreme sentimentality.

Jesus called his followers together and went off to the lake. A large contingent from Galilee followed. Many came from Judea, Jerusalem, Idumea, and the regions on the other side of the Jordan and around Tyre and Sidon. They had heard about all the things he was doing. The crowd was so large that he told his followers to get a small boat ready. He wanted a little distance from the crowd. He had cared for so many sick people that those with physical problems were nudging their way forward just to touch him.[3]

When unclean spirits saw him, they dropped down at his feet and screamed, "You are the son of God." But he gave them a strong warning, telling them to keep quiet about who he was.[4]

He went up a mountainside and beckoned certain followers he had picked out, and they joined him. He had selected twelve to be with him and to go out and represent him and teach. They also had the authority to deal with the demonic forces. The twelve[5] were: Simon (called Peter), James the son of Zebedee and his brother John (called Boanerges, or Sons of Thunder), Andrew, Philip, Bartholomew, Matthew, Thomas, James son of Alphaeus, Thaddeus, Simon the Zealot, and Judas Iscariot, who betrayed him.

Jesus went into a house, and once again a crowd pressed on him so that he was unable to eat. When his close friends got wind of the situation, they came in to bring things under control. Some people were saying that he was out of his mind.[6]

7   Another reference to Jesus's connection to demons. The point may be obvious: If you are related to the realm of invisible presences, you will know both the powers of light and the powers of darkness.

8   Now we see Jesus accused of having an evil spirit himself. But it is only natural that if someone is miraculously healing people he will appear as more than human, and people might see him as possessing either good or bad powers. There is also something frightening about the display of such powers. That fear can easily turn into anger.

9   "We shall not dignify with a response attempts by Church writers, early or late, to prove James and Jesus had different mothers or, depending on their theological position, different fathers. We shall take these for what they are, embarrassment over the existence of Jesus' brothers and bids to protect the emerging doctrine of the supernatural [Christos]."
    —Robert Eisenman, *James the Brother of Jesus: The Key to Unlocking the Secrets of Early Christianity and the Dead Sea Scrolls* (New York: Penguin, 1997), 9

10 As you enter the state of mind represented by the image of the kingdom of God in Mark—an attitude of genuine humility and service—your sense of belonging changes. You no longer identify in a narrow way with your family's values but expand toward a universal, global sense of belonging and familial connection. Jesus's words about his own family are not necessarily harsh, but signal this shift to a larger feeling of belonging.

11 "The more nobly a [person] wills and acts, the more avid he or she becomes for great and sublime aims to pursue. He will no longer be content with family, country, and the remunerative aspect of his work. He will want wider organizations to create, new paths to blaze, causes to uphold, truths to discover, and an ideal to cherish and defend. So, gradually, the worker no longer belongs to herself. Little by little the breath of the universe has insinuated itself into her through the fissure of her humble but faithful action, has broadened her, raised her up, borne [her] on."
    —Pierre Teilhard de Chardin, *The Divine Milieu* (New York: HarperCollins, 2001), 37

The lawyers from Jerusalem said, "He's possessed by Beelzeboul. So he's effective in dealing with demonic possession because of his association with the head demon."[7]

Jesus called the people to him and spoke in parables. "How can Satan get rid of Satan? A kingdom divided against itself cannot stand, and neither can a house. If Satan works against himself and is split, he cannot stand. It's all over. No one can break into a strong man's house and steal his things unless he first ties the person up. Then he can rob the house. I assure you, people will be pardoned for all their wrongdoing and blasphemies, but whoever desecrates the Holy Spirit will never be pardoned. His guilt is eternal."

He said this because they had claimed he had an evil spirit.[8]

Jesus's mother and brothers arrived. They were standing outside and sent someone in to notify him. Some people were sitting next to him and said, "Your mother and brothers are outside. They're looking for you."[9]

"My mother and brothers? Who are my mother and brothers?"[10] Gazing at the people around him, he said, "Here are my mother and brothers. Whoever fulfills God's wishes is my brother and sister and mother."[11]

1   Ancient traditions refer to Jesus as a new Orpheus. Early paintings in the
    catacombs show him with a large lyre, a symbol of Orpheus. He is the poet-
    visionary who charms with his stories and teachings.

    "Just as Orpheus tamed wild beasts with his music, his image became the
    image of [Christos] who, with his words, transformed the lives of sinners."
        —Umberto Utro, "Vatican Hopes Crowds Visit Sarcophagi Museum," *Catholic
        News Service* (October 3, 2005). www.religionfacts.com/christ-as-orpheus

2   A parable is not exactly a teaching story or a moral fable. In the Gospels, it is
    a story that, in John Dominic Crossan's words, "shatters your complacency."
    It is like a parabola, a word to which it is related. It takes you out on a prom-
    ising path and then brings you back to a point farther away from where you
    began and from the world you know. Again, Crossan says that it "keeps the
    world free of its idolatry and open in its uncertainty."
        —John Dominic Crossan, *In Parables: The Challenge of the Historical Jesus* (Sonoma,
        CA: Polebridge Press, 1992), 27

3   "Jesus did not impose the reign of God upon his hearers. He merely let it
    show itself. The responsibility for seeing and hearing rested entirely with
    them: who has ears to hear, let him hear. And each person was free to enter
    in upon that reign in accordance with his ownmost destiny."
        —Robert Funk, *Jesus as Precursor* (Philadelphia: Fortress Press, 1975), 92

4   The word for "mystery" in Greek is *mysterion*, meaning not a problem to solve
    but an important reality too profound to easily put into words. A mystery is
    not a hole in our understanding; it is a positive presence that is not meant
    to be understood. We can respond to it creatively without knowing much
    about it. Birth is a mystery in many ways; we do not understand it fully, but
    we celebrate it and write about it. Jesus's vision for humanity is also a mys-
    tery, asking more for response than explanation.

5   Isaiah 6:9–10.

Chapter 4

Once again he began teaching at the lake. The crowd grew to such numbers that he got into a boat on the lake and sat down.[1] The crowd remained on the shore. He put many thoughts in parables,[2] as when he said, in the middle of his teaching, "Listen to this. A sower went out to sow. As he sowed, some seed fell on the road and birds came and ate it. Other seed fell on stony ground with little topsoil. It was planted shallow and so it sprouted quickly. But when the sun rose, it shriveled up, since it had no roots, and withered away. Other seed fell among shrubs that sprouted and smothered it and so it yielded no grain. Other seed fell on good soil and produced good grain, increasing thirty, sixty, and a hundred times."

Jesus said, "If you're listening, pay attention to this."[3]

When they were by themselves, the twelve and others were curious about the parables. He said, "To you I present the mystery of the kingdom of God.[4] But to those outside, I speak in parables so that

> *Seeing, they see but don't grasp,*
> *Hearing, they hear but don't understand,*
> *Otherwise they would change and be pardoned."*[5]

6   The Gospels make this point again and again. The message and the king-
    dom itself are tiny, in a sense, and yet they can generate a whole world of
    creativity and vitality. Once you get the simple idea of life lived from a dif-
    ferent fantasy altogether, one based on *agape*—love and respect—everything
    changes. If you can accept this idea, like the earth receiving a seed, then the
    results will be far, far greater than you could ever expect.

7   The seed is one of several images that depict the kingdom not as something
    in itself but a catalyst. You sow the seeds of love, neighborliness, friendship,
    imagination, and healing, and the kingdom grows up out of this.

       The new way of being, the kingdom of the sky, is like a seed. You do not
    do anything to make the seed grow into grain. It just happens. You plant the
    seed and then you harvest the grain. Planting, waiting, and harvesting are
    three phases of life in the kingdom. You can trust that living in the new man-
    ner of the Gospels will lead to a fruitful life

8   The mustard seed is perhaps the most remarkable image in the Gospels. It is
    so tiny, and this is the best image for what the kingdom is—not a worldwide
    movement but a microcosmic change in attitude that alters the world. We
    need seeds of change more than we need lengthy explanations or huge insti-
    tutions. A small community of seekers might be more effective than a huge
    congregation.

       John Dominic Crossan has a different take on this image. The mustard
    plant is a fast-growing weed that threatens the work of farmers, as do the
    birds that make nests in it. This, according to Crossan, is a metaphor for the
    kingdom.
       —John Dominic Crossan, *Jesus: A Revolutionary Biography* (San Francisco:
          HarperSanFrancisco, 1989), 64–65

    Jesus is a threat to the conventional world that is full of injustice, self-
    aggrandizement, and conflict.

Jesus said, "Don't you get this parable? If not, how will you understand any parable? The farmer sows the teaching. Some people are seeds along the road where the teaching is scattered. They hear it but then Satan appears, like that, and steals the teaching that had been planted in them.

"Others, like seeds sown on stony areas, hear the teaching and receive it happily right away. But these seeds have no roots and last just a short time. When trouble or threat comes along because of the teaching, they are soon frustrated.

"Others are sown among shrubs. They hear the teaching but cares of the world and the lures of wealth and various cravings come along and smother the teaching and they bear no fruit.

"Others are like seeds planted on good soil. They hear the teaching, take it in, and it produces fruit that is thirty, sixty, and a hundred times what was planted.[6]

"When you get a lamp, do you put it under a bowl or a bed? No, you put it on a pedestal. See, there is nothing secret that will not be revealed, nothing hidden that will be not be made visible. Hear what I'm saying. Take note of it.

"Listen carefully: To the extent you give, to that extent you will be given—even more so. If you have, you will be given more. If you do not have, whatever you have you will lose.

"The kingdom of God is like a person scattering seed in the earth. Night and day, whether he's asleep or awake, the seed sprouts and grows. He may not understand how. The soil makes grain all on its own—first the stalk, then the head, then the grain. When the grain is ready, he goes at it with his scythe—it's harvest time.[7]

"What is the kingdom of God like? What can I compare it to? It's like a mustard seed, the tiniest seed you can plant in the earth.[8] Once planted, it expands and becomes the largest of all garden plants and has such large branches that birds from the sky build nests in its shade."

9 This is an important sentence to guide us in our reading of the Gospels. The translation of the Greek is literally, "Except in parable he did not speak to them." How should we interpret this sentence? Does Jesus really say nothing to the people that is not a parable? Should we then treat everything as a story or as having a poetic meaning? There are several instances in the Gospels where Jesus seems frustrated with his students' tendency to miss the metaphor in his teaching. In the Sophia of Jesus Christ, one of the Gnostic gospels, he laughs about that.

10 Why was Jesus not worried? First, remember that this is a story, not history. It could be a story about being in the midst of a stormy life or a turbulent situation—in your personal life, in your family, or in society. We all know stormy times only too well. Because Jesus has amazing trust, he can sleep peacefully through the storm. We need that kind of calm and can get it if we live the kingdom style of life.

11 If we take this miracle as a sign, we might reflect on Jesus's teaching as having an impact on the natural world. Currently, Western culture seeks to subdue and control nature in direct, technological ways. Commentators often judge Gospel miracles by the standards of Newtonian physics, saying that a miracle like this proves Jesus's divinity. They fail to take into account the poetic, spiritual elements that are at the heart of Jesus's teaching. As poetry, this passage suggests that the Jesus way has the power to keep the world calm and make it less dangerous.

Jesus taught them with many parables like these, as many as they could handle. He said nothing to them that wasn't a parable.[9] But when he was alone with his followers, he explained everything.

One day, evening was coming on and he said to them, "Let's go to the other side." They left the people behind and took him in the boat he was in. Other boats joined them. A turbulent squall came up and waves swept over the boat and almost swamped it. Jesus was in the back of the boat, sleeping on a cushion. The students woke him up. "Teacher, aren't you worried that we'll drown?"[10]

He got up, hushed the wind, and shouted to the waves, "Quiet. Calm down." The wind died down and a great calm descended.

He said to his followers, "Why are you so jittery? Are you still lacking in trust?"

They were terrified and said to each other, "Who is this? The wind and the waves obey him."[11]

1   It is common today to think that people of Jesus's time did not have our sophistication to understand mental illness as a personal condition, or even as a disease. They spoke of someone like this man having an unclean spirit that possessed him. But more recently, as in the work of psychologist James Hillman, we see the value in recognizing and personifying the inner personalities or complexes that, on the negative side, cloud our awareness and make us behave erratically. Hillman speaks of them as "powers."
   —James Hillman, *Re-Visioning Psychology* (New York: HarperCollins, 1975), 191, 225

From a positive perspective, the cathartic spirits are the inspirers that guide us and make us creative.

2   We sometimes speak of the devil or Satan, as though there is only one single unclean spirit. But each of us has many powers urging us into life, some of them unclean because of a long history of violence and abuse, some evil because there is a dark side to life. We are still fighting wars of centuries ago, and those ancient spirits still haunt us. The powers that move us onward are many, and our task is to sort them and give each one attention. For example, you may have to get to the bottom of your chronic anger or your racial prejudice. What are the unclean spirits that disrupt the harmony of your life?

Chapter 5

They crossed the lake to the region of Gerasenes. Jesus got out of the boat just as a man with an unclean spirit came up from the graveyard to meet him. The man lived among the tombs and they couldn't keep him tied him up any longer, not even with a chain. Earlier they had secured his hands and feet, but now he broke the chains and the irons on his feet. No one had the strength to restrain him. He would yell out night and day among the tombs and in the mountains and cut himself with stones.[1]

When he saw Jesus at a distance, he ran and fell down in front of him. With a screeching voice, he shouted, "What do you want with me, Jesus, son of the high God? Swear by God; don't torment me."

Jesus said, "Depart from this man, unclean spirit."

Then Jesus asked him, "What's your name?"

He answered, "My name is Legion—we are many." He begged Jesus not to expel him from the region.[2]

3   The pig is associated with Mother Earth, her womb, and her children. It is
     also connected to the "wandering womb disease," or hysteria. The pig as
     earth and human body offers a temporary home for unclean spirits that then
     disappear beneath the surface of the water.
          —Erich Neumann, *The Great Mother*, trans. Ralph Manheim (Princeton, NJ:
              Princeton University Press, 1963), 189

Yogic literature also suggests that some spirits, troublesome and out of
control, need a container like the earth to control their volatility. We have
to be careful not to take out our frustration on animals or the natural world
or even culture by making it ugly. On the other hand, we could consider
where our unclean spirits have gone and deal with them more directly.

     Carl Jung says that our complexes can be found in the things of the world
around us, even in our heating systems.
          —C. G. Jung, *Dream Analysis: Notes of the Seminar Given in 1928–1930*, ed. William
              McGuire (Princeton, NJ: Princeton University Press, 1984), 265

They are also in our unconscious, in our drive to care for the natural world,
to protect our children, and to treat animals with dignity.

4   A poignant detail: The man with the demon asks to go with Jesus in his boat.
     Another sign of the close connection between Jesus and the more-than-
     human, even if this is the dark side of that equation. There is a mysterious
     intimacy between Jesus and the demonic. This suggests that Jesus is not a
     mere wisdom teacher but someone in touch with the mysterious. Of course,
     we see this also on the bright side with his intimacy with the Sky Father. But
     being connected to both light and dark points to a full spiritual realization
     on the part of Jesus.

     In another way, the man's wish to be close to Jesus is understandable, but
     it is never good to be too close to the raw power of life. You have to keep
     a distance, even from Jesus, allowing him his separate reality and not cozy-
     ing up to him as a familiar. Devotion is important, but sometimes devotion
     becomes too personal and intimate. Maybe it is not a good idea to get in the
     boat with Jesus after all.

On a nearby hillside a large herd of pigs was grazing. The spirits begged Jesus, "Send us into the pigs. We want to go into them."[3]

He did their bidding and the unclean spirits exited the man and entered the pigs. The herd, about two thousand, rushed down the steep bank into the sea and drowned. The herdsmen ran off and told the story in the town and countryside and the people went out to see what had taken place.

When the people reached Jesus, they saw the man who had been possessed by Legion, sitting there, clothed and in control of his faculties, and they were struck with fear. Those who had seen what happened to the demon-haunted man told the others about it. They mentioned the pigs as well. The people then encouraged Jesus to leave their area.

Jesus was just getting into the boat when the man who had been demonically possessed asked to go with him.[4] Jesus said no. "Go home to your family and friends and tell them how much the teacher did for you and how kind he was to you. So the man went home to DeCapolis and told the story of all that Jesus had done for him, and the people there were in awe.

5   The number twelve is prominent in this passage: twelve years of bleeding,
    a twelve-year-old girl. Twelve is the fullness of time giving rise to change.
    Both Johann Sebastian Bach and Igor Stravinsky used it in music as a build-
    ing block. Every time we buy a dozen eggs or a dozen doughnuts, we can
    remember how often the number twelve structures our world, as in the
    twelve months and the twelve tones in a chromatic scale. Why not thirteen
    eggs? Or fourteen?

6   This mysterious detail further complicates the image of Jesus. We have seen
    him as someone who interacts with unclean spirits, and here we are shown
    that his power to heal is somehow in him and yet apart from him. Appar-
    ently, he heals by a power that radiates from him. This phenomenon distin-
    guishes ancient culture from our own modern one. We do not imagine that
    we have powers in us that can have an effect in the world. We want total
    subjectivity. If we do something, we do it. When Jesus does something, by
    contrast, a power in him accomplishes the deed. If we want to learn from
    Jesus, maybe we could discover powers to heal within ourselves that are also
    somehow separate from us.

7   It is noteworthy that the woman took the initiative to find a cure. Jesus
    does not know what happened. He is looking for her in the crowd. He is
    a source of healing, but does not have to know that he is doing it. Another
    lesson: When we are sick, we may want to go looking for a source of healing
    power—a doctor or some other kind of healer—but we can participate in
    our own healing. We tend to view healing power as medical skill, which is
    quite a different thing.

When Jesus had again crossed the lake by boat, he encountered a large gathering by the water. A synagogue leader named Jairus was there, and when he saw Jesus he bowed down at his feet and begged him sincerely, "My young daughter is about to die. Please come and place your hands on her so that she will be all right and live."

Jesus left with him.

A massive group of people followed and huddled around him. A woman who had had hemorrhages for twelve years was among them.[5] She had tried many doctors and had spent all the money she had but was no better. In fact, she was worse. When she heard Jesus, she pushed through the crowd and touched his garment, thinking, "If I can only graze against his clothes, I'll get better." Immediately the source of her bleeding closed up and she could feel in her body that she was finally free of her affliction.

Instantly Jesus sensed that power had gone out of him and he turned around to the people and asked, "Who touched my clothes?"[6]

His followers responded, "In this mass of people? How can you ask, 'Who touched me?'"

Jesus scanned the crowd to catch a glimpse of who had done it.[7]

The woman, nervous and fearful, knowing full well what had happened inside her, approached and bowed down in front of him and told him the truth.

"Daughter," he said. "Your trust has cured you. Go now, and don't worry. Be relieved of this illness."

As he was talking, some people came from the house of the leader of the synagogue with the news that his daughter was dead. "Don't disturb the teacher again," Jesus's followers told them. Overhearing their rebuke, Jesus said, "Don't give in to fear, just have trust."

8 "The mourners' laughter seems quite inappropriate given the seriousness of the moment.... Commentators on Mark often assume that the girl is indeed dead, although Mark does not say this—in fact, Jesus asserts the contrary.... Yet it seems rather improbable that the family should mistake sleep for death. If the girl is dead, this miracle of her resurrection is comparable to Jesus's raising of Lazarus."
—George Aichele, *Jesus Framed* (London: Routledge, 1996), 65

9 Some scholars think this is a magical formula; others, a term of endearment. Maybe, with the translation "lamb," it refers to Jesus as the good shepherd taking care of his people, especially the young.

10 This is one of many instances where Jesus, moved by simple kindness, thinks of food. If you were to list the many times food comes up in the Gospels as a form of service, you would be surprised. Other spiritual traditions, such as Buddhism, are mindful of the importance of food as sustenance for the body as well as the soul and spirit. Everything Jesus does in this part of Mark comes with overwhelming kindness. It does not seem right to interpret the food as proof of his powers. On the other hand, we can consider food as a metaphor for nourishment of soul and spirit.

He didn't let anyone go with him except for Peter, James, and John the brother of James. They arrived at the leader of the synagogue's home and found pandemonium, people crying and moaning. He went in and said, "Why the big commotion and the wailing? The child isn't dead. She's just sleeping." The mourners laughed.[8]

He sent them out and led the girl's father and mother and friends in where the child was. Holding her hand he said, "*Talitha koum*, that is, get up, little lamb."[9] Instantly the girl got up and walked (she was twelve). The people there were overcome. But he instructed them firmly not to say anything to anyone and then suggested that they give the little girl something to eat.[10]

1   We come across this astonishment on the part of Jesus's listeners often. Where does he get his talents and powers? These passages give the impression of someone from another place or gifted with powers that are unusual and awe-inspiring. At the same time, he is a local. People know his family. It is important to keep this special quality of Jesus in mind so as not to think of him as a mere teacher. His genius is real and extraordinary. He is always, at least in part, in the sphere of the mysterious, and people are frequently amazed at his abilities. This amazement may suggest that life in the kingdom is indeed amazing in many ways. There may be powers available there that are not accessible in the reality we know.

2   Notice that he does not talk about belief, but rather simple trust. The Gospels share with Taoism and other traditions a basic trust in the bountifulness of life. Whether you experience religion as an institution or as a personal state of being depends on whether you emphasize allegiance to a creed or deep trust. Why does trust have so much power? For one thing, it helps get the ego out of the way, allowing alternate powers to emerge and do their work.

3   A small detail in passing, but again we see how Jesus's students are also each Christos, anointed, made special by the oil that signifies profound and essential change. If you model your life on that of Jesus, the messiah, the man of oil, you live differently, taking on the challenge to love and respect others, even your perceived enemies. The oil sets you apart with special powers and mission.

Chapter 6

He left there and went with his followers to his home country. On the Sabbath he taught in the synagogue and astonished those in attendance. "Where did he get all this knowledge and what is this wisdom that has given him so much power? Isn't he just a carpenter? Isn't he the son of Mary and the brother of James, Joseph, Judas, and Simon? Aren't his sisters here with us?" People found the whole thing confusing. [1]

Jesus said, "In his hometown and among his relatives and even in his own house a prophet has no honor."

He couldn't do his wondrous deeds there. He only laid his hands on a few sick people and tended them. He was astonished at their lack of trust. [2]

He went out to the villages, teaching. He summoned the twelve and sent them out two by two and gave them power over unclean spirits. He instructed them to carry nothing with them on their way, maybe only a walking stick—no bread, no pouch, no money in their belts. "Wear sandals but don't bring an extra tunic. If you enter a household, stay there until you leave the town. If a place won't welcome you or listen to you, shake the dust off your feet when you leave as a sign of your displeasure."

They went out and taught people to change their way of seeing things. They expelled demonic forces from many people and put oil [3] on them and cared for them.

Jesus was becoming well known and King Herod got wind of it. Some said that John, the one who baptized, had risen from the dead and that's why Jesus had special powers. Others said he was Elijah. Some thought that he was a prophet like one of the old ones.

4 Although the story of John the Baptist's beheading has historical backing, as a Gospel story, rich and captivating, it also has mythic, symbolic and theological meaning. John makes the first move toward the new kingdom, a utopian vision for humanity. A powerful king kills him hideously because of a dance, a girl and her mother. The mother hates John because he doesn't accept the validity of her marriage. Sex lies in the background. Perhaps John has not reconciled sexuality and spirituality, as Jesus does later. His vision, symbolized by his head, prepares for Jesus but is shown to be itself inadequate.

When Herod considered all this, he concluded, "It's John, the one I beheaded. He's come back from death."[4]

Herod had given the order to arrest John, put him in shackles, and keep him in prison. It was all because of Herodias, his brother Philip's wife, whom he himself had married. John had told Herod, "It isn't legal for you to have your brother's wife." For that reason, Herodias felt deep antipathy toward John and wanted to kill him. But she couldn't. Herod was afraid of John and shielded him. He knew that John was an ethical and holy man. When Herod heard him speak, he was confused and yet enjoyed listening to him.

The crucial day came when Herod celebrated his birthday by putting on a dinner for military leaders and leading figures in Galilee. Herodias's daughter arrived and danced and impressed Herod and his guests. The king said, "Ask for anything you'd like and I'll give it to you." He swore, "Whatever you wish will be yours, up to half of my kingdom."

She left and consulted with her mother, "What should I ask for?"

"John, the one who baptized. His head," her mother said.

The young woman rushed back to the king. "I want you to give me the head of John, the one who baptized. Now. On a plate."

The king was quite upset. But he couldn't very well refuse her in the face of all his promises and in the presence of his guests. So immediately he called for the executioner and ordered him to bring John's head in. The man went and beheaded John in prison and brought the head back on a plate. He offered it to the girl, who gave it to her mother.

When they learned about all this, John's followers came and got the body and laid it in a tomb.

5   Jesus's followers express the practical, frugal view, recommending that they
    encourage the people to go into the towns to eat. But Jesus is different,
    in tune with his vision for a new kingdom. He wants to feed the people
    in his own way. The five loaves of bread and the two fish, among other
    things, again demonstrate that the kingdom is not big. It is nourishing in the
    extreme, but it is tiny compared to the impact it can have on individuals and
    society.

6   Jesus groups the people in numbers and in organization. He creates a little
    society right there. The numbers may well be symbolic. For a fresh discus-
    sion in terms of sacred geometry, see David Fideler's book, *Jesus Christ, Sun
    of God: Ancient Cosmology and Early Christian Symbolism* (Wheaton, IL: Quest
    Books, 1993), 109–124.

7   It is worth noting these moments when Jesus is alone, since most of the
    time he seems to be in the company of his friends and students. You can
    read every word and gesture of Jesus as a mudra, a symbolic sign of how the
    way of life he teaches is to be lived. The Gospels are not ordinary stories of
    everyday life in Galilee. They are more like sacred works of art, showing in
    great detail the nature of Jesus's vision. They are full of symbol, metaphor,
    and image, and have to be read as poetry, rather than as narrative. They are
    closer to prose poetry than to history or biography.

Those who had been sent out to teach gathered around Jesus and gave him their news about what they had done and taught. Then, since so many people were coming and going, not giving them enough time even to eat, Jesus said, "Come with me, just ourselves, to a quiet place where we can get some rest."

They went away by themselves by boat to a place that would be quiet. But some of the people recognized them as they were leaving. These people ran on foot through all the towns and got to the destination first.

When Jesus disembarked and saw the massive throng of people, he was concerned about them. They were like sheep without a shepherd and so he taught them many things. It was getting late and the followers came and said, "This is a godforsaken place and it's late. Send these people away so they can go to nearby country places or towns and get some food."

"No," he said. "Give them something to eat."

"We would need eight months of a person's earnings to get enough food. Should we spend that on bread so they can eat?"[5]

"See how many loaves of bread you have."

They checked and said, "Five—and two fish."

Jesus suggested that the people sit in clusters on the grass, and they did—in groups of hundreds and fifties.[6] He picked up the five loaves of bread and the two fish and looked up to the sky, said a blessing, and broke the bread. He presented the pieces to his followers to pass around to the people. He also divided the two fish among them all. Everyone ate their fill. The followers picked up twelve baskets filled with bits of bread and fish. Five thousand people had eaten.

Urgently Jesus told his followers to get into the boat and cross to the other side to Bethsaida. He dismissed the people and then left and went up on a mountainside to pray.

By evening the boat was in the middle of the lake and he was on land, alone.[7] He watched the students work hard at rowing—the wind was against them. It was around the fourth

8   The students, it seems, are terrified at seeing Jesus. This could be the fright
    one might feel at seeing something uncanny, unnatural. Throughout the
    Book of Mark there is a building sense of an essential difference between
    Jesus and his followers. They are ordinary humans, but he is almost like a
    member of another species. Walking on the water, he is like a sea creature.
    They do not know who it is until he tells them, "Hey, it's me."

9   This is a mysterious passage. What do they not understand? And why does
    feeding the crowd make their hearts hard? Later there is a hint that maybe
    the event is actually a story, and the students do not understand the met-
    aphors and symbols. Or perhaps, as they often do, they take it all liter-
    ally instead of metaphorically. Some commentators say the students do not
    understand that the teaching is meant for Gentiles as well as Jews. Others
    say that the scene is an enacted parable, and the students miss the point.
    Could it be that Jesus is always immersed in the life of the kingdom, where
    bread is a sacred symbol for eating together in friendship? The students do
    not understand this because they have not yet embraced the rhetoric of the
    kingdom. As many people do, they resist the suggestion that actions can be
    symbolic, rather than naturalistic.

10 This touching is a kind of *darshan*, being in the presence of the teacher and
    receiving healing power from it. It is significant that a story like this one
    shows the importance of an effort to be present, rather than an intellectual
    agreement with a set of teachings. Many people who love the Gospel stories
    have not had the full experience because they have been taught to think of
    them as the basis for a creed rather than a way of being. Even in our reading,
    sometimes our ideas and beliefs get in the way of feeling the impact of the
    Gospels as story. We might think of reading them as a kind of *darshan*, where
    the reading itself puts us in touch with the power of the story.

watch of the night and he went out to them, walking on the water, and almost passed them by. When they saw him walking on the lake, they thought he must be a phantasm. They all saw him and were afraid and screamed.[8]

He spoke to them then: "Take heart. It's me. Nothing to fear." He climbed into the boat with them and the wind died down. They had been completely stunned by the miracle of the bread. They didn't understand it and their hearts were not soft.[9]

They completed the crossing and landed at Gennesaret and dropped anchor. As they were getting out of the boat, people there recognized Jesus. They scoured the region and brought the sick on stretchers to wherever rumor had it he was. Wherever he went—villages, towns, or countryside—they put the sick down in the squares and begged him to allow them to touch just the edge of his garments. Everyone who touched him got better.[10]

1   Jesus's relationship with the Pharisees is complicated. Historically, a great
    number of commentators have described it in ways that connect it to the
    widespread and dangerous idea that Jews were and are responsible for Jesus's
    execution. I recommend the writing of theologian John T. Pawlikowski,
    OSM, who portrays the Pharisees as good models for our own contempo-
    rary spiritual lives. See, for example, John T. Pawlikowski, "The Pharisaic
    Revolution—Its Significance for Christian Renewal," *Notre Dame de Sion*.
    www.notredamedesion.org/en/dialogue_docs.php?a=3b&id=1200.

    I also recommend the works of George W. E. Nickelsburg, an emeritus
    professor of religion, who writes, "However innocent some Christian typol-
    ogizing [branding without historical subtlety] may have been over the cen-
    turies, we have learned after Auschwitz how it has been put to demonic use."
    —George W. E. Nickelsburg, "Review of Anti-Judaism in Christian Theology
    by Charlotte Klein," *Religious Studies Review* 4, no. 3 (July 1978): 161

2   Isaiah 29:13. The old way is to go through the motions of cleanliness, while
    the new way of Jesus is to be clean inwardly, to have a soul transformed by
    real catharsis. As many have pointed out, religious purity can serve a good
    purpose or it can get out of hand. This is not a condemnation of the Phari-
    sees as such, but a warning against extreme, legalistic purity in any tradition.
    Remember, Jesus is spelling out a clear description of what the kingdom of
    the sky can be.

3   The word "corban" means "near," and came to mean an offering in Jesus's
    time. Here it is used cleverly to sidestep support for parents. This passage
    is not directed against the Pharisees but against anyone who uses legalistic
    arguments to avoid fulfilling a basic human duty and to suppress any feeling
    of guilt about refusing to take that action.

Chapter 7

Pharisees and clerks from Jerusalem came to him and saw his followers eating bread with polluted, unwashed hands. Following ancient traditions, Pharisees and Jews generally wash their hands carefully or they don't eat. Nor do they eat when they're just back from the market, unless they first wash their hands. They have other traditions, too: ritually washing cups and pots, pitchers and tables.[1]

The Pharisees and lawyers asked Jesus, "Why don't your followers observe the old traditions instead of eating bread without washing their hands?"

Jesus responded, "Isaiah was right. He predicted your hypocrisies:

> *These people praise me with their lips*
> *But they are far from me in their hearts.*
> *They worship me in a void*
> *Teaching their own ideas*
> *as if they were divine.*[2]

"You cling to human ways and abandon the ways of God. Moses said, 'Honor your father and mother. Whoever curses his mother and father should be put to death.' You hold that if a person says to his mother or father, 'Whatever aid you expected from me is corban,[3] a gift assigned to God,' he no longer has to give anything to his parents. But your practice contradicts the word of God. And then you do many things like this."

4 This statement still holds true today: Eating unapproved food is not in itself going to make you a bad person, unfit for the kingdom. It is what is in you and comes out of you that makes all the difference. If you tell lies, manipulate people, or take care of yourself at the expense of others, it makes no difference what kind of religious diet you observe. Who you are and what you do places you in the kingdom—or not. Still, despite this warning, traditional practices can be full of life and meaning.

5 I suggest that we look more deeply into what has long been called "casting out demons." When I was growing up, I often heard people say of someone fighting alcoholism, "He's dealing with his demons." The Greek word here, as is usually the case, is *daimon*, which is not the same as "demon." It can be good or bad, and it has the connotation of being an inner urge. So, yes, we have to come to terms with certain overwhelming and potentially destructive urges. That achievement is one of the tasks required to enter the kingdom of the sky.

6 In her own way, this Greek woman expresses the all-important point of view of the kingdom: It is for everyone, not just a special group with a special history. Jesus wants to transform the world, not just reform a religion. The story could be about an atheist. Such a person has access to the healing power of the kingdom, if he or she grasps the main idea of the shift in how you see the world. This is captured in the Greek word *metanoia*, often translated moralistically as "repentance." But the word consists of *meta*, as in "metamorphosis," a radical change, like the one from caterpillar to butterfly, and *noia*, "knowledge" or the order of the world. *Metanoia* is therefore a deep change in the way a person understands the world.

7 Here a genuine expression of humility and an egoless concern for a child allow healing to take place. When a person's heart is in the right place, Jesus responds. An interior purity of intention leads one into the kingdom, where healing comes naturally.

Jesus gathered the people closer to him and said, "All of you, listen and try to understand. Nothing outside of a person can make him unclean by going into him. It's what comes out of a person that makes him unclean."[4]

He left the people and went into the house and the followers asked him about the parable.

"Are you slow?" he asked. "Don't you see how nothing going into a person from the outside can make him unclean? It doesn't enter his heart. It goes into his stomach and then out and into the toilet. So all the food is clean.

"What comes out of a person makes him unclean. Sexual indulgence, theft, murder, adultery, greed, wickedness, deception, lewdness, envy, slander, haughtiness, and folly come from inside, from people's hearts. All these horrible things come out and defile a person."

Jesus left there and went to the region of Tyre. He slipped out of a house without being seen, but then the word got out. As soon as she heard that Jesus was around, a woman whose daughter was demon-haunted came and bowed down at his feet. She was Greek, of Syrian-Phoenician descent. She asked him to expel the demonic force from her daughter.[5]

"First, let the children have anything they want to eat. It's wrong to take a child's bread and toss it to the dogs."

"Yes, sir," she said. "But the dogs under the table might still eat the children's crumbs."[6]

He told her, "Because you've said this the demon has left your daughter." She went home and found her child lying in bed, the demonic force gone.[7]

Then Jesus left the Tyre region and went through Sidon, down to the Sea of Galilee and into the area around the DeCapolis. There, some people brought him a man who was deaf and could hardly talk. They asked him to put his hand on the man.

8   Throughout the Gospels Jesus refers to the sky as an image for the realm of power and mystery. He speaks of his Father in the Sky and the kingdom of the sky. The sky breaks open, and a voice speaks.

9   There are many stories in the Gospels about healing ears and eyes, clearing them out so that a person can see and hear. In some cases, Jesus makes it clear that the hearing and seeing are not only physical. We may hear many words without truly hearing what is being said. We may see a lot of life without seeing through to its deeper significance. To be in the kingdom requires more than the usual powers of perception.

As the poet William Blake notes, "If the doors of perception were cleansed, every thing would appear to man as it is, infinite."
    —William Blake, "The Marriage of Heaven and Hell," *The Complete Poetry and Prose of William Blake*, ed. David V. Erdman (Berkeley: University of California Press, 1982), 39

We also have to learn how to speak powerfully.

Jesus led him away from the crowd and placed his fingers into the man's ears. Then he spit and touched the man's tongue. He looked up to the sky[8] and said with a deep sigh, *"Ephpha-tha."* which means "to open up." At that moment the man's ears cleared up and whatever was binding his tongue loosened and he spoke clearly.[9]

Jesus instructed them not to tell anyone. But the more he tried to keep them quiet, the more they broadcast the news. People were in awe. He's good at everything. He makes the deaf hear and the speech-impaired talk.

1   Here is another central quality of Jesus that teaches a lesson about the king-
    dom: He is capable of deep emotion. The Greek word is *splanchnizoamai*,
    meaning "deeply moved." We have an unusual English word, "splanchnic,"
    that refers to the intestines. As used here, the word suggests feelings deep
    in the gut; not superficial. Sometimes spiritual teachers present compas-
    sion as though it were a matter of mind, understanding the community of
    humankind. Sometimes they accent the heart. Here it is the gut, the belly.
    In that deep, intimate way we can be open to the needs of others.

2   The history of religion is full of tales in which people sought or demanded
    proof for claims and teachings. Typically, we understand the Gospel miracles
    as proof of Jesus's divinity and power, proof that he is worthy of our faith.
    But Jesus has no patience with this approach. Faith is not built on proof, but
    on trust.

Chapter 8

Again a great crowd formed and had nothing to eat. So Jesus summoned his followers and said, "I have deep feeling[1] for this mass of people, for they have been here with me for three days and have eaten nothing. If I ask them to go home, they'll faint on the road—some have come a long way."

His followers said, "How can we give all these people bread here in the desert?"

"How much bread do we have?" Jesus asked.

"Seven loaves."

He told the people to sit down and then he picked up the bread and offered thanks and broke it up and asked his followers to pass it out among the people. They had a few tiny fish, as well. Jesus blessed these and asked that they, too, be passed around.

The people ate and were full. They picked up the leftovers and filled seven baskets. And about four thousand people were there. He asked them to leave and then got into a boat with his followers and traveled to the district of Almanutha.

Pharisees showed up and argued with him. To test him, they asked for a sign from the sky. He let out a sigh and said, "Why do these people demand a sign? I assure you, no sign will be given to them."[2] Then he left and got into the boat and crossed to the other side.

The followers had forgotten to bring bread and had only a single loaf in the boat. He warned them, "Be careful. Be cautious around the yeast of the Pharisees and Herod." One of them said, "I guess he's talking about us not having any bread."

3   Jesus's teaching demands that we hear what is said at a deep level that is not literal and plain, but poetic. In this case, for example, the *story* of the bread and fish is not only a miraculous tale of transformation of substances but also a symbolic statement about the kingdom.

4   The real miracle is akin to the story of the mustard seed. It takes a small shift in thinking to live the Jesus way of life, and that new imagination needs to be fed; thus the bread and fish. Jesus himself said that he—the vision he embodies—is the bread of life. We also see in several instances that people shifting to the new vision are fish, caught by the Jesus vision.

    The numbers here are also interesting and probably symbolic: Twelve usually represents the twelve tribes of Israel and therefore the old law; seven, the gentiles and the new law; and four, the ordinary world in which we live.

5   Commentators offer many explanations for the saliva. A simple one that makes sense to me comes from my memory of my mother moistening a handkerchief with her tongue, when I had a scratch, to begin the healing. This was far more than a physical aid, since I felt the care coming from my mother when her saliva touched my skin.

6   This charming detail of the walking trees helps get away from the idea of Jesus's healing as a presto, abracadabra, instant miracle. It feels more like a natural process put into motion by Jesus's caring actions. We also have to remember to read these stories on many levels at once, not getting stuck on one way of understanding them. If this healing is a parable in action, then the blindness may be not only physical but also psychological. We may be so stuck in the materialistic worldview of our time that we are blind to higher, deeper, and more sublime ways of seeing. Furthermore, entering the kingdom is a process and may involve phases over time. You do not necessarily see what life is all about in a flash.

Jesus overheard this remark and said, "What is this about not having bread? Don't you get it? Are your hearts calloused? Do you have eyes but can't see? Do you have ears and yet are hard of hearing?[3] Don't you remember? When I divided the five loaves of bread for five thousand people, how many baskets of leftovers were there?"

"Twelve," they said.

"And seven for four thousand. How many baskets of leftovers?"

"Seven," they said.

"Do you still not get it?"[4]

They arrived at Bethsaida, where people presented a blind man and begged Jesus to touch him. He led the blind man out of town, put saliva on his eyes, and placed his hands on him.[5]

"Can you see anything?" he asked.

The man squinted and said, "I see people, but they look like walking trees."[6]

So Jesus put his hands on the man's eyes once again. The man looked around hard and saw things clearly. His eyesight had come back. Jesus told him to go away without entering the village.

7 The man of oil is someone who resides in an exalted state, who has achieved what everyone is looking for and working toward. Jesus is a kind of bodhisattva, someone who has reached a level of realization symbolized by the utopian kingdom of the sky but remains in the ordinary realm to help people do well in life and strive toward their own realization. Oddly, this status threatens many people, so Jesus has to be wary of revealing his true identity.

8 Jesus does not advocate a herd mentality in which we all submit to one doctrine and authority. We each have to take up our own cross, shoulder the weight of our own lives, and in that condition reach for the utopian vision of Jesus. This is what I have called "a religion of one's own," living out our own fate in community with all beings of the earth.
   —Thomas Moore, A Religion of One's Own: A Guide to Creating a Personal Spirituality in a Secular World (New York: Avery, 2014)

9 Do you pay constant attention to your soul, or do you instead just try to amass all possible material rewards of life? To neglect your soul is to court unhappiness and a meaningless life. At the same time, to care for your soul you may have to experience loss, which causes you to feel more deeply and to reflect constructively on your experience. Loss is one of the ways in which the soul gains depth. Several paradoxes are at work here.

10 If you insist on clinging to the usual worldly values, you will be embarrassed if you find yourself in a situation where the kingdom is in place, where the highest spiritual values and strong compassion of the heart are fully in play. This is the realm symbolized by the Sky Father and the beings of the sky, angels.

Jesus and his followers toured the villages around Caesarea Philippi. As they walked he asked them, "Do people talk about who I might be?"

"Yes. Some think you're John, who baptized; some think you're Elijah or one of the prophets."

"And you? Who would you say that I am?"

Peter answered, "You're the man of oil."

Jesus asked them not to say anything about this.[7]

He informed them that the son of man would endure many trials and be spurned by the elders, chief priests, and lawyers. He would also be killed and then three days later would rise. He was crystal clear about these things, and Peter complained.

Jesus gazed at his followers and scolded Peter.

"Back off, Satan. You're not thinking about God's interests. You're focused on the human side of things."

Then he signaled for the crowd and his followers to come close. "If someone wants to join me, he has to pick up his own cross,[8] forget about his worries, and follow me. If someone wishes to save his soul, he will have to lose it. If someone loses his soul for me, he'll save it. What use is it to acquire the entire world and give up on his soul? What could a person possibly give up for his soul?[9]

"If my teaching embarrasses some member of this adulterous and misguided people, then when that person arrives in the magnificence of his father and his angels, he will embarrass the son of man."[10]

1   "The transfiguration of Jesus was witnessed by devotees who had extin-
    guished their personal wills, men who had long since liquidated 'life,' 'per-
    sonal fate,' 'destiny,' by complete self-abnegation in the Master... [Such a
    person], his personal ambitions being totally dissolved, no longer tries to live
    but willingly relaxes to whatever may come to pass in him; he becomes, that
    is to say, an anonymity. The Law lives in him with his unreserved consent."
        —Joseph Campbell, *The Hero with a Thousand Faces* (New York: MJF Books,
          1949), 236–237

2   This is another striking instance in which a voice comes from above, in this
    case from a cloud. Here the mysterious speaker assures everyone that the sky
    itself approves, affirms, and indeed loves Jesus and his work. That is to say,
    Jesus is not just a social reformer or a teacher of wisdom. He has a strange
    and wonderful intimacy with the highest and most mysterious source of life.
    His role is not just worldly but spiritual as well.

Chapter 9

Ican truthfully say that there are some here now who will not die before they see that the kingdom has fully arrived in all its power.

Six days later Jesus took Peter, James, and John up a high mountain all alone. In their presence he was transformed. His clothes shone with a blinding light—no one could have made them whiter. They saw Elijah and Moses talk with Jesus.[1]

Peter said, "Rabbi, it is good for us to be here. Let's make three tents for you, Moses, and Elijah."

Jesus didn't know how to respond, seeing them so frightened.

But then a cloud spread over them and a voice intoned, "This is my son, my beloved. Listen to him."[2]

Suddenly they looked and saw only Jesus and no one else.

As they were coming down the mountain, he told them not to tell anyone what they had witnessed until the son of man had risen from the dead. They did, in fact, keep it all to themselves, but they wondered what "risen from the dead" could possibly mean.

They asked, "Why do the experts in the law say that Elijah has to come first?"

"Yes, Elijah is coming first to renew everything. Why is it predicted that the son of man has to suffer so much and be treated so badly? All I can say is that Elijah came, and, as predicted, they did to him whatever came into their minds."

3   This talk about spirits causing problems may sound archaic, but it still goes
    on today. We simply have different language and concepts for it. Many
    people have skin problems, speech impediments, and so on because of
    some "spirit" that entered them at a crucial moment. Freud talks about these
    issues as "conversion hysteria." A wound to the psyche often manifests as a
    physical illness.

4   This is one of the most beautiful lines in the Gospels. We do trust, but still
    we need help trusting. We have good intentions and we do our best, but
    sometimes that is not enough. We discover through failure and setbacks that
    our trust is not as strong as we would like it to be. Then is the time simply
    to pray, not naively but intelligently, expressing our dependence and limi-
    tations. This alone can transform the soul and educate it to a level where
    power returns.

Returning to the community, they saw a big gathering of people, including some experts in the law, in a heated discussion. When the people saw Jesus, they got excited. They were awestruck and ran to greet him.

He said, "What's the argument all about?"

A voice from the crowd yelled out, "Teacher, I brought my son. He has a spirit in him that has taken away his power of speech. When it takes hold of him, it pushes him down and he foams at the mouth and grinds his teeth and becomes stiff. I asked your followers to get rid of this spirit, but they couldn't do it."[3]

He responded, "You people don't trust enough. How much longer do I have to be with you and deal with all this? Bring him here."

They brought the boy to them. When the spirit caught sight of him, instantly it threw the little one into convulsions. He fell on the ground and rolled around and foamed at the mouth.

Jesus asked the boy's father, "How long has this been going on?"

"Since he was a child. Sometimes it throws him into fire and water, trying to kill him. If you can do anything, kindly help us."

"A person who trusts can do anything."

The boy's father suddenly pleaded, "I do trust. But help me with my lack of trust."[4]

When Jesus saw that the people were running to look at what was going on, he scolded the unclean spirit. "Deaf and speechless spirit," he said, "I order you to exit and never enter this boy again."

The spirit screeched, threw the child into violent convulsions, and exited. The boy looked like the living dead, so much so that people said, "He's gone." But Jesus grabbed his hand and lifted him up and he stood on his feet.

Once Jesus had gone inside the house, his followers inquired, "Why couldn't we drive this thing out?"

"You can expel that kind only through prayer," he said.

⚬

5   This is one of the key inverted values we find in the Gospels. If you have a
    desire to achieve and lead and be at the top of the pile, you have to be last
    and serve. We find similar sentiments in Taoism and Zen Buddhism. Zen
    master Shunryu Suzuki says, "Sometimes the disciple bows to the master;
    sometimes the master bows to the disciple. A master who cannot bow to his
    disciple cannot bow to Buddha."
        —Shunryu Sukuki, *Zen Mind, Beginner's Mind* (New York: Weatherhill, 1973), 44

6   These lines sound as if they come from the Gosepl of John, such as John 8:29
    and 14:6–7, where Jesus often comments on his father's realm, which is quite
    alien and mysterious. Embrace a child and you are touching the kingdom
    beautifully embodied. Invite the Jesus way into your life and you invite in
    the realm where Jesus comes from, a mysterious level apart from our cor-
    rupted world that we can only glimpse and hope for.

7   A key aspect of Jesus's teaching is inclusiveness. Do not feel that you live
    among the chosen and the righteous. Anyone anywhere on the planet, with
    any background or point of view, can be part of the Jesus kingdom. It is not
    a club but a community of people united by their vision and way of life. For
    centuries this point has been lost on many who call themselves the followers
    of Jesus but do not understand the universality of the kingdom.

8   Perhaps based on an historical place of refuse and fire, Gehenna came to
    mean a place of destruction and torment, something like hell.

9   The kingdom of heaven is a loving community. We depend on each other.
    Because we are radically connected in this kingdom, if someone causes
    another to be misled or to do the wrong thing or to go down a misguided
    path, the responsibility is severe. Jesus offers one strong image after another
    to make his case for responsible communal living.

They left there and walked through Galilee. Jesus wanted their whereabouts to be secret because he wanted to teach his followers. He told them, "The son of man will be betrayed into the hands of some people. They'll assassinate him, but in three days he'll rise." They didn't understand what he was saying and were hesitant to ask him about it.

When they arrived at a house in Capernaum, he asked them, "What were you discussing on the road?" They didn't say anything because they were debating about who was the greatest among them. He sat down and invited the twelve to sit with him.

"Anyone who wants to be first has to be last—and everyone's servant, too."⁵ He put a small child in their midst and held it in his arms. "Whoever embraces a child like this in my name embraces me, and whoever welcomes me doesn't welcome just me but the one who sent me."⁶

John said, "Teacher, we saw someone driving out a demonic power in your name and we tried to stop him because he isn't one of your followers."

Jesus said, "No, don't stop him. If someone exercises a power in my name, he won't speak poorly of me afterward.⁷ Whoever is not against us is for us. If anyone gives you a glass of water because of your connection to the man of oil, he will certainly not be without his reward.

"If anyone causes a single one of these ordinary persons who put their trust in me to make a misstep, it would be better to have a millstone hung around his neck and for him to be tossed into the sea. If your hand makes you lapse, cut it off. It's preferable to be an amputee than to have two hands in Gehenna⁸ and eternal fire. If your foot makes you lose your way, cut it off. It's preferable to be lame than to have two feet in Gehenna. If your eye makes you stumble, gouge it out. It's preferable to enter God's kingdom with one eye than to have two eyes in Gehenna, where the worm never dies and the fire never goes out.⁹

10 Salt is one of several images for the intensification of life you find in the kingdom. There, you live at a different level. Salt is similar to oil in this regard.
Both represent qualities that raise ordinary life up many notches, to the
level where meaning and real love are possible. Psychologist James Hillman
describes salt as substance, value, and fervor. It gives you tenacity and vital-
ity, although it can become extreme and take the form of fanaticism. "Too
little and principles go by the board; too much and a Reign of Terror ensues."
> —James Hillman, "Salt: A Chapter in Alchemical Psychology" in *Salt and the
> Alchemical Soul*, ed. Stanton Marlan (Woodstock, CT: Spring Publications,
> 1995), 173

Carl Jung also commented on Mark's reference to salt: "Here salt undoubt-
edly means insight, understanding, wisdom.... For this purpose a flexibility
of mind is needed."
> —Carl Jung, *Mysterium Coniunctionis*, vol. 14, *The Collected Works of C. G. Jung*, trans.
> R. F. C. Hull (Princeton, NJ: Princeton University Press, 1970), par. 325

"The fire there will roast everyone.

"Salt is good, but if salt loses its tang, how can you restore its saltiness? Have salt[10] in yourself and be peaceful with each other."

1   Today many people take divorce for granted and just ignore this teaching of Jesus. It may sound moralistic and old-fashioned, but seen as part of the entire Gospel teaching, it may indicate that if we could truly inaugurate the utopia of the sky kingdom—not pic in the sky but an intelligent alternative to the life we have created—then divorce need not be an option. Even now, some people get divorced thinking that it is nothing more than the dissolution of a contract. Then they get sick and cannot sleep, and dream for years about their lost spouse. Deep in the soul, divorce is usually not an easy thing. We should not take it lightly.

There is also a tendency in divorce to blame your partner for the dissolution of the relationship, as a way of protecting yourself from the deep, heavy feelings of responsibility and choice. Jesus's words lend divorce a degree of seriousness that is rare in our time. Besides, forbidding divorce is not nearly as strong as pointing to its weight on the soul.

Chapter 10

Jesus left and went to the region of Judea beyond the Jordan. Large masses of people again surrounded him and he taught them.

Some of the Pharisees showed up to test him. "Is it legal for a man to divorce his wife?" they asked.

"What did Moses say?"

"Moses allowed a man to divorce his wife and leave her."

"Moses wrote this law because hearts were blocked. At the beginning, God made them male and female. This is why a man will leave his mother and father and embrace his wife, the two becoming one body. They are no longer two, but one. What God has put together no human being should separate."

When they were in the house once again, the followers asked Jesus about all this. He said, "Anyone who divorces his wife and marries another woman commits adultery. If she divorces her husband and marries another man, she commits adultery."[1]

2   Jesus tells many stories about outsiders and misfits being more likely to merit inclusion in the kingdom than people who think of themselves as virtuous. But the issue goes even deeper. Children belong because they do not fit in the adult world. They have different ways of thinking and relating to others and to the world. They are good candidates for the kingdom. And that is not just because of their innocence, but also because of their uncontrolled passions. Jesus seems to be saying that if adults could embrace the mentality of children, they would more likely find their way to the kingdom.

3   This is a clear expression of the radical demand of the Jesus revolution. It is not enough to do the basics, to avoid bad behavior. You have to create a radical sense of community and step back from pure self-advancement. It is difficult, if not impossible, for someone to pursue financial wealth as the main goal in life and still be part of the kingdom.

4   Take this comparison at face value. It is impossible to fully enter the Jesus kingdom while you are focused on gaining material wealth. This is not to say that wealth is automatically an obstacle, but it is if it interferes with your responsibility to respect everyone, live a life of healing, and keep all demonic urges at bay.

5   In the kingdom it is absolutely necessary to have a vision that penetrates through and beyond worldly values. The sky is your image. You need to be in touch with values and a worldview that is not limited to this-world expectations. You have to break through to higher values.

6   This is true. They leave everything at a moment's notice to join Jesus in his mission and remain loyal to him. In the Gospels they are known as followers and students; rarely are they called apostles. They empty themselves to learn the Great Teaching. Churches seem more interested in filling adherents with lessons than in promoting emptying, but this passage would calls for a different approach.

Some people brought children to Jesus so that he could hug them, but his followers chided them for doing that. When Jesus saw this, he wasn't happy and said, "Let the children come to me. Don't stand in their way. They are natural citizens in the kingdom of God.[2] Anyone who can't be like a child can't enter the kingdom." He held a child in his arms and put his hands on her in blessing.

As Jesus was walking on a road, a man ran up to him and got down on his knees and said, "Kind teacher, what should I do to merit eternal life?"

"Why call me kind? Only God is kind. You understand the commandments: Don't murder, commit adultery, steal, lie, or cheat. Honor your father and mother."

"Teacher, I've done all this from childhood."

Jesus gazed at him and felt affection for him. "There's one thing you haven't done," he said. "Go, sell everything you own and give it to the poor. Then your treasure will be up there. Then you can come and join me."[3]

When he heard this, the man became depressed. He had many possessions.

Jesus looked around and told his followers, "It isn't easy for the wealthy to enter the kingdom of God."

His followers were confused. Jesus repeated, "It's a challenge for the rich to enter the kingdom of God. It would be easier for a camel to pass through the eye of a needle than for a wealthy person to enter the kingdom of God."[4]

Jesus's followers were again stupefied. "Then who can ever be saved?"

Jesus looked at them and said, "At the human level it is impossible, but with God anything can happen."[5]

Peter added, "We have given up everything to join with you."[6]

"I can assure you that anyone who has left behind his home or children or property, or his brothers and sisters and mother

7   This statement should be a challenge to those who enjoy the world's pres-
     tige and material rewards: "The first will be last." Jesus says that it is possible
     to have worldly power and gain and still be in the kingdom, but it is difficult.
     The task for a member of the Jesus kingdom is not to increase your sense of
     self but to become more sophisticated in your devotion to others. Paradoxi-
     cally, a life of service grounds the self and gives life purpose, healing many
     emotional wounds along the way.

8   This reference to baptism suggests that it is far more than a rite of member-
     ship. It is a difficult passage to a new level of experience, nothing less than
     the ritual form of *metanoia*, a profound change in vision that is difficult to
     achieve and that has serious repercussions. The sacrament is next to mean-
     ingless without the passage.

9   Once again we see how radically different the sky kingdom is from ordinary
     ways of life. In the new dispensation, leadership means service. It does not
     imply entitlement, ease, self-aggrandizement, or control over people. Lead-
     ership is the understanding that everyone else comes first. The leader's job is
     to serve.

and father, for me and for the gospel will have a hundred times all of this now and eternal life in the future. However, he will be persecuted as well. But many who are first will be last, and the last first."[7]

They were going up the road to Jerusalem with Jesus leading the way and were full of awe, while those who followed were afraid. He set the twelve aside and explained what was going to happen to him.

"We're going to Jerusalem, where the son of man will be handed over to the chief priests and lawyers. They'll sentence him to death and give him over to the masses. They'll taunt him and spit on him and flog him and execute him. Three days later he'll wake up."

James and John, the sons of Zebedee, approached him and said, "Teacher, we would like to ask something of you."

"And what is that?"

"Let one of us sit at your right hand and one at the left in your splendor."

"You don't know what you're asking for. Can you drink the cup that I drink? Can you go through the baptism[8] that I am going to go through?"

"Yes, we can," they said.

"You'll drink my cup, all right, and you'll be baptized in my baptism. But it isn't up to me whether you sit at my right and left. That is for those it was designed for."

When the other ten heard all this, they got angry at James and John. Jesus brought them together and said, "You know well that among the masses their leaders abuse them and people in high places lord it over them. It's different with you. Whoever would like to be in a high position among you must be your servant. Whoever wants to be first has to be in the service of everyone.[9] Even the son of man did not come to be served, but to serve, to give his life as a ransom for many."

10 Another reversal: a rejected blind beggar becomes a model for being in the kingdom. Scripture scholar Wendy Cotter makes this point forcefully:

> Bartimaeus is the incongruous ideal for the listener. The narrator is saying that Jesus saw in Bartimaeus the most admirable conviction and unshakeable resolve. Yet, the behavior that expressed it completely conflicts with what is considered refined and worthy of praise. Even Bartimaeus himself, from the bottom rung of society, is held up by Jesus as a model.
> —Wendy Cotter, *The Christ of the Miracle Stories: Portrait through Encounter* (Grand Rapids: Baker Academic, 2010), 74

11 After a series of radical statements about the challenge of joining the new kingdom, we have a moving story of being able to see after being blind. Understand this as a condition of a person's worldview and not just as physical sight. You have to develop a new kind of vision altogether to join with Jesus in his fate and enter the new kingdom.

They were in Jericho, just leaving the city in fact, and surrounded by a mass of people, as a blind man, Bartimaeus, son of Timaeus, sat by the side of the road begging. When he discovered that Jesus was passing, he called out, "Jesus, son of David, show me kindness."

Some of those present chided him and told him to keep quiet. But he shouted out even louder, "Son of David, be kind enough to help me."

Jesus stopped. "Bring him over here."

They spoke to the blind man, "You'll feel better now. He's asking for you. Get up."

Taking off his shawl, Bartimaeus got up and approached Jesus.

Jesus asked him, "What do you want from me?"

He said, "I want my sight."

Jesus said, "Go on then. Your trust has made you better."[10]

Instantly he got his sight back and joined Jesus on the road.[11]

1   Scholars will tell you the historical background for this detail about the unridden horse, but think of it as an image in its own right. The whole point of Jesus's teaching is to live by an entirely new philosophy built on communal love and respect, *agape*. As he comes now into the public eye, he appears fresh, free of the past, a new being, just like his animal.

2   Again, a small point, but Jesus gets his horse from the people. His teaching is all about creating human community that knows no physical or political boundaries. People in the street are happy to cooperate with his entry into public life.

3   Psalm 118:25–26.

4   Again and again we are told that the kingdom is arriving, that it is almost here. Today we are in the same situation. The values that Jesus taught have not yet been brought to fruition. His kingdom is still "almost here."

5   The word "highest" is central to Jesus's teaching. He is active in the lowliest ways among people and lives a simple earthly life, but his teaching is from the sky, from the highest place. It is sublime, transcendent, and divine.

6   "Mark himself knows that Jesus was not just purifying but symbolically destroying the Temple, because he carefully framed his action within the fruitless fig tree's cursing and its withering. As the useless fig tree was destroyed, so, symbolically, was the useless Temple."
    —John Dominic Crossan, *Jesus: A Revolutionary Biography* (San Francisco: HarperSanFrancisco, 1994), 131

7   Isaiah 56:7.

8   Jeremiah 7:11.

Chapter 11

They drew closer to Jerusalem and arrived at Bethphage and Bethany, near the Mount of Olives. Jesus told two of his followers to go into the village and find a colt that has never been ridden.[1] "Untie it and bring it here. If anyone asks why you're doing this, tell him, 'The master needs it and will return it soon.'"

They went off and found a colt outside in the street, tied to a gate. As they were untying it some people nearby said to them, "What's going on? Why are you freeing the colt?" They told them what Jesus had said, and the people let them take it.[2]

Then they brought the animal to Jesus and threw some garments on it. Jesus sat on it. People then spread their coats on the road, or branches they had cut from trees. Then people at the head and others in back chanted:

> *Hosanna!*
> *Praise the one coming*
> *in the name of the Lord.*[3]
> *Praise the realm of our forefather David*
> *That is almost here.*[4]
> *Hosanna in the highest.*[5]

When he entered Jerusalem, he went into the Temple and chased out the ones buying and selling things there.[6] He flipped over the tables of those exchanging money and selling doves, and prevented anyone from carrying things through the Temple. He reminded them that it was written,

> *My house will be known as*
> *A house of prayer*
> *for all nationalities,*[7]
> *But you have made it*
> *A den of thieves.*[8]

71

9   It is interesting that in this paragraph trust and forgiveness come together. There is something about trusting people and life itself that puts you in a position where you can forgive. Both indicate an open heart and a flow between you and the world.

10 This is another typical instruction for meriting a place in the kingdom: Your heart has to be clear. The word is "catharsis." You have to be free of regrets and resentments. Cleaned. Cleared out.

When the chief priests and clerks heard this, they began to look for a way to kill him. They were afraid of him, because the whole populace was in awe of his teaching. When evening came, Jesus and his followers left the city.[9]

In the morning they passed a fig tree all dried up. Peter remembered and said, "Rabbi, look. The fig tree you cursed has dried up."

Jesus said, "Trust God. If you say to a mountain, 'Rise up and be tossed into the sea,' and if you have no doubt in your heart and trust that it will happen, what you wish for will be done. Whatever you ask for in prayer, trust that you'll get it, and it will be yours. When you stand to pray, if you have something against another person, be forgiving, so your father above will forgive you your mistakes."[10]

They returned to Jerusalem and as he was talking in the Temple, the chief priests and clerks and elders approached and challenged him. "What is your authority for doing these things? Who gave it to you?"

"Let me ask you a question," he responded, "and I will tell you about my authority. Was John's baptism from above or from a human source? Tell me."

They discussed the question. "If we say from above, then he'll ask us why we didn't trust it; if from human origins ..." They were afraid of the people, who believed John was a prophet. So they said to Jesus, "We don't know."

Jesus said, "Then I won't tell you where I get the authority to do what I do."

1 Of course, Jesus is the badly treated son. Whoever represents the kingdom should be prepared for rejection, and worse. Offering a healing message is one side of the Christos archetype, but being rejected and treated badly is the other.

2 Psalm 118:22–23.

Chapter 12

That day he began speaking in parables.

"A man planted a vineyard, put hedges around it, dug a hole for the winepress, and erected a tower. He leased it to tenants and went on a long journey to another country. When harvest time arrived, he sent a servant to the tenants to collect produce from the vineyard. But they roughed him up, beat him, and sent him away empty-handed.

"So he sent another servant. They treated this one with contempt and threw stones at him and gave him a wound to the head. He sent yet another, and they killed him. He had one person left, his beloved son, whom he sent, thinking, 'They'll show some respect to my son.' But, of course, the tenants thought, 'This is the son, the heir. If we do away with him, we'll inherit everything.' So they grabbed him, killed him, and threw the body outside the vineyard.[1]

"What do you think the owner would do? He would come and bring those tenants to ruin and give the vineyard to someone else. Have you ever read this quote?

> *The stone the builders reject*
> *Becomes the cornerstone.*
> *The Lord's doing*
> *And astonishing in our eyes."[2]*

When they realized that the parable was about them, they wanted to arrest him, but were concerned about all the people. So they left and went on their way.

Then a few Pharisees and Herodians were sent to catch him in his teaching. They approached and said, "Teacher, we are aware that you teach with sincerity and aren't afraid of anyone. You don't worry about anyone else's agenda and teach God's

3   As is usually the case, when faced with options, always choose all of them, not one. Find a way to be in a poly-modal world, where many different claims are made on you. If someone forces you into a choice, he is most likely manipulating you. If you remain undecided, you lose your personal power. If you choose one over the other, you simply escape from the complexity of life. Dealing directly with complexity gives you richness of soul.

4   Exodus 3:6.

way honestly. Is it legal to pay taxes to the emperor or not? Should we pay them?"

Fully aware of their hypocrisy, he replied, "Why do you test me? Hand me a denarius. I'd like to look at it." They gave him one. "Whose image is on this? And whose logo?"

"Caesar's."

"Give Caesar what is Caesar's and God what is God's."

They were impressed.[3]

Sadducees came to him with a question. Note that they don't speak of the resurrection.

"Teacher, Moses left us instructions: If a man's brother should die and leave his wife behind, but no children, the brother should embrace the wife and have children for his brother. Once there were seven brothers. The first got married and then died and left no children. The second one married her and died without any children. Same with the third. In fact, none of the seven had any children. Finally, the wife died. Now, in the resurrection, when they've all risen, of the seven whose wife will she be?"

Jesus responded. "You don't understand, and you don't appreciate either the scriptures or God's power. When they rise from the dead, they'll neither get married nor already be married. They'll be like angels.

"Now about the dead rising, have you ever read in the book of Moses that God spoke to him in the bush and said,

"I am the God of Abraham, Isaac and Jacob?"[4]

"He is not the god of the dead, but the god of the living. You're simply wrong."

A lawyer arrived and heard the discussion. Observing that Jesus had responded well, he asked, "Of all the commandments, which is first?"

5   Deuteronomy 6:4–5. These verses are known in Judaism as the *Sh'ma*, the oldest and most important of Jewish daily prayers.

6   Leviticus 19:18. While Jesus asks you to "take up your own cross," at the same time he calls for radical community. This brief quote from the Hebrew Bible suggests a truly profound definition of communal consciousness. You understand how each of us is unique and yet shares basic human emotions, thoughts, and responses. "Share" is not quite the word. Another's experience is so like our own, disregarding differences in history and personality, that one wonders if in some way we are not all one person. In "The Over-Soul," Ralph Waldo Emerson writes, "I live in society; with persons who answer to thoughts in my own mind, or express a certain obedience to the great instincts to which I live."
     —Ralph Waldo Emerson, "The Over-Soul," in *The Portable Emerson*, ed. Carl Bode (New York: Penguin, 1981), 215

7   "The transcendental is not infinite and unattainable tasks, but the neighbor who is within reach in any given situation."
     —Dietrich Bonhoeffer, *Letters and Papers from Prison* (New York: Macmillan, 1972), 381

8   This simple sentence offers a good hint about the nature of the kingdom. This lawyer, part of a group that is often criticized in the Gospels, is not far from the kingdom simply because he understands the two dimensions of a godly human life: love of the divine and love of the human. Just knowing this, and presumably living it out, brings him nearer the kingdom.

9   Psalm 110:1.

Jesus said, "This one is first in order of importance:

> *Listen, Israel, the Lord God, Our Lord, is one.*
> *Love the Lord your God*
> *with your whole heart and soul*
> *and mind and ability.*[5]

"The second commandment is similar:

> *Love whoever you encounter as yourself.*[6]

"No commandment is more important than these."

"Well done, teacher," the lawyer said. "It's true, as you said, that God is one and there is no other and to love him with your whole heart and soul and mind and ability and to love whoever you encounter as yourself—this exceeds all burned gifts and sacrifices."[7]

When Jesus heard his thoughtful words, he told him, "You are not far from the kingdom of God."[8]

After that no one bothered him with questions.

As Jesus was teaching in the Temple, he said, "How can the experts in the law say that Christos, the man of oil, is a son of David? David himself said, through the holy spirit:

> *The Lord said to my lord,*
> *'Sit to the right of me*
> *until I place your adversaries*
> *beneath you.'*[9]

"David himself refers to him as 'Lord'; so how can he be his son?"

The crowd enjoyed this exchange.

10 A psychological aspect of living in the kingdom is to see through literal
   events to their deeper significance. Here Jesus sees a larger truth in the widow's action—it is not the quantity of money that makes the difference but
   what that money represents in the life of the giver. There is something psy-
   choanalytic, in a general sense, about life in the kingdom, an appreciation
   for deeper motives and underlying narratives. Jesus's references to Jewish
   history and religious ideas and leading figures also work as an archetypal
   psychology, appreciating grand figures and themes that shed light on the
   present.

As part of his teaching, he said, "Be cautious around the experts in the law who like to wear long robes and enjoy being recognized in the markets and want the best seats in the synagogues and high places at festivals. They consume widows' properties and make a show of praying for a long time. They will be judged severely."

He sat down opposite the box for offerings and watched people put their money into it. The rich tossed in their riches. A poor widow came along and deposited two tiny copper coins, a penny's worth. He motioned to his followers to join him.

"This penniless widow has contributed more than anyone else. They all gave from their riches, while she in her poverty put in everything she had, her very livelihood."[10]

1   How will we know when the kingdom of the sky is almost in place? Now it seems that it might be centuries before this utopian vision will be accepted and lived. But will there be violent conflict between the two worlds, the worldly and the utopian? People are invested in both, and currently it appears that the great majority are preoccupied with the worldly.

2   As many commentators point out, the kingdom has begun but is far from established in the world. We still have wars and rumors of war, indications that the kingdom is still not fully realized. But we also see signs of community, healing, compassion, and occasionally miraculous peace making.

Chapter 13

O n the way out of the Temple, one of the followers
observed, "Teacher, look at the style of stonework and
the building methods here."

Jesus said, "See these huge buildings? Not a single stone will
be standing on top of another. It will all fall down."

Sitting at the Mount of Olives opposite the Temple, Peter,
James, John, and Andrew asked Jesus quietly, "Can you tell us when
this will happen? Will there be some sign that the time has come?"[1]

Jesus said, "Don't let anyone mislead you. People will come
forward using my name and claim, 'I am the one.' They will con-
fuse people. When you hear of wars and rumors of wars, don't
get excited. All this has to happen, but the end is not here yet.
A country will rise up against other countries, kingdom against
kingdom. Everywhere there will be earthquakes and famine. All
this is just the beginning of the birth pangs.[2]

"Be cautious. They'll turn you in. They'll beat you up in the
synagogues. Because of me you'll be handed over to rulers and
kings to testify against me.

"All countries will hear about the Great Teaching first.

"When they turn you in and bring you to court, don't worry
ahead of time what you should say. Just say whatever comes to
you at that moment. Not you, but the Holy Spirit will be speaking. Brother will betray brother to the death, and a father, his
child. Children will rise up against their parents and have them
put to death. Because of my name, everyone will despise you.
But if you get through to the end, you will be safe.

"When you behold the disgusting horror there, where it has
no right to be (please, try to understand), if you are in Judea,
run to the mountains. If you are on your rooftop, don't go
down into the house. Don't go inside your house to retrieve

3   Sometimes it is difficult to distinguish between the oil of transformation and
     snake oil. Jesus is recommending a very sharp sense of discernment, an abil-
     ity to distinguish the merely beguiling from the transformative. One of the
     greatest problems in contemporary spirituality is emotional gullibility linked
     with intellectual weakness. Too many too easily fall into spiritual movements
     not worthy of them.

4   Unconsciousness and intellectual and moral lethargy are among the main
     problems in finding your way into and staying in the kingdom. Many spiri-
     tual stories tell of the problem of being sleepy and not alert. You have to
     stay awake and not slip into old, lazy habits. Ordinary life lived according to
     the ways of the world is a condition of sleep—Newton's sleep, says the poet
     William Blake.
     —William Blake, "Letter to Thomas Butt, 22 November 1802," in *The Complete
       Poetry and Prose of William Blake*, ed. David V. Erdman (Berkeley: University of
       California Press, 1982), 722

     The kingdom requires an alert mind. You have to know what is going on in
     your world and resist the tendency to slide and drift on currents that flow
     away from the kingdom's core tenets.

5   This is a common theme in spiritual literature. The Buddha is known as
     "the awakened one." One of Johann Sebastian Bach's most stirring can-
     tatas is *"Wachet auf"* ("Wake Up"). The renowned religion scholar Mircea
     Eliade makes an interesting comment on the spiritual tradition of waking
     up: "Since Gilgamesh's adventure it has been well known that conquering
     sleep, remaining "awake," constitutes the most difficult initiatory ordeal, for
     it seeks a transformation of the profane condition."
     —Mircea Eliade, *A History of Religious Ideas*, vol. 2 (Chicago: University of
       Chicago Press, 1982), 336

     Gilgamesh was asleep when a snake came and snatched away the plant that
     would have granted him immortality. You could say that *metanoia* is a waking
     up and shifting out of the "profane condition." It is an interesting thought:
     To be asleep is to be unaware of the sacred.

something. If you're in a field, don't go back for a shirt. It will be really bad at that time for anyone who is pregnant or nursing.

"Pray that your escape doesn't occur in the winter. There will be suffering then of a scope not seen from day one of creation up to now, or even in the time to come. If the Lord hadn't cut these days short, no bodies would be spared. He lessened the time for the sake of the chosen ones.

"If someone tells you that Christos is over there or over here, don't believe him. A pseudo-Christos and pseudo-prophets will appear.[3] Wherever they can they'll do wonders and signs intended to charm even the chosen ones.

"Pay attention and do what I say. There, I've given you a warning.

"Then, after all that upheaval, the sun will grow dark and the moon won't shine. Stars will fall out of the sky and the planets will stop orbiting. People will see the son of man coming in a mist with awesome power and majesty.

"He will send his angels and summon his chosen ones from the four directions, from pole to pole.

"Consider the parable of the fig tree: When her branches get moist and produce leaves, you know that summer is on its way. In the same way, when these things happen, know that the time has come and the end is just about to unfold.

"I'm telling you honestly, this generation won't move on until all of this comes to pass. The earth and the sky may pass away, but my words won't. No one, not the angels, not the son, but only the father knows the day and the hour.

"Stay awake and pray, because you don't know when the time has come. The son of man is like a person who took a long trip. He left his house and instructed his servants and handed out assignments and told the gatekeeper to keep a watchful eye.

"Be alert.[4] You don't know when the master of the house will come—in the evening, at midnight, at dawn, or in the later morning. Don't risk him coming and finding you asleep. I can say only this to one and all: Stay awake."[5]

1   Once again we see Jesus as the man of oil. Only, here, a woman anoints him,
which he thinks is a special gift. He gives us another lesson about the kingdom: Frugality is not always the appropriate attitude. There are times when
expensive, sensual, and extravagant attention is appropriate. He adds the
element of death and burial, indicating that her action prefigures his execution. I also see in this use of oil an indication of Epicurean tendencies in
Jesus, an appreciation for occasional pleasure and luxury. It is not the norm
in his lifestyle, but he defends it.

Chapter 14

Two days before Passover and the Festival of the Unleavened Bread. The chief priests and experts in law are looking for a way to take Jesus quietly into custody and assassinate him. But not during the festival, they say, or the people might revolt.

Meanwhile, Jesus was in Bethany at Simon's house. While he was sitting at table, a woman came in with an alabaster jar full of expensive oil made from flowers of spikenard. She opened the jar and dribbled the oil on his head.[1] A few of those present were indignant, "Why did she waste that oil? She could have sold it for more than three hundred denarii and given the money to the needy." They went on scolding her.

But Jesus said, "Leave her alone. Why do you give her such grief? She did something special for me. You'll always have the poor around, but you won't always have me. You can always help the poor anytime. She did what she could. She anointed my body for burial. I predict that whenever the gospel is spread around the world, what she has done will be recounted as a memorial to her."

2   Judas is an important character in the story of Jesus. He gives a face to betrayal, alerting us to the shadow side of spiritual commitment. Peter's betrayal is a character flaw, but Judas's kiss and the financial reward he receives for his betrayal take us into the pit of ruin. He is one of the twelve, that magic number of perfection, now shown to be imperfect.

3   This vignette about finding the room for the Last Supper adds a touch of humanity to the portrait of Jesus. It shows him capable of making simple arrangements for a dinner—reinforcing his Epicurean nature—while at the same time inserting a degree of mystery in preparation for a sacred meal, one that will be replicated millions of times throughout history.

4   "[In earlier magical texts] a magician-god gives his own body and blood to a recipient who, by eating it, will be united with him in love … a Dyonysiac parallel to the eucharist, but not its source."
    —Morton Smith, *Jesus the Magician* (San Francisco: HarperSanFrancisco, 1978), 123

5   You can find a beautiful song sung by Jesus and his followers in the Acts of John, a second-century CE collection of traditions focused on the apostle John, part of the Christian Scriptures.
    "The Acts of John describes an initiatory ceremony in which Jesus' 12 disciples, representing the constellations, perform a dance around their master, who represents the pole star at the center."
    —Timothy Freke and Peter Gandy, *Jesus and the Lost Goddess: The Secret Teachings of the Original Christians* (New York: Harmony, 2001), 114

One of the twelve, Judas Iscariot, went to the chief priests and betrayed Jesus.[2] They listened and were happy and promised him money, and then he planned how he might successfully carry out the betrayal.

On the first day of the Festival of the Unleavened Bread, when people would kill the Passover lamb, Jesus's followers said, "Where do you want us to prepare the Passover meal?"

He dispatched two of them, saying, "Go into the city. You'll see a man carrying a carafe of water. Stay behind him. Where he goes, you go and tell the main servant of the house, 'The master asks, "Is there a dining room where I can eat the Passover meal with my followers?"' He'll show you a large upper room, furnished and set out. Get ready for us there."[3]

His followers entered the city and found just what he had said they would and prepared the Passover.

In the evening, Jesus came with the twelve. They sat and ate and Jesus said, "You know, one of you eating with me will betray me." They were sad and one by one asked, "Is it I?"

He replied, "Yes, it is one of you twelve, the one who dips into the dish with me. The son of man has to experience what was written about him, and yet the one who betrays him would be better off if he had never been born."

They ate and Jesus took bread and blessed it and broke it apart and gave it to them, saying, "Take. This is my body." He took the cup and gave thanks and handed it around to them and they all drank from it. He said, "This is my blood of the new paradigm. It is shed for many people. I have to tell you that I will not drink the fruit of the vine again until I drink it in a new way in the kingdom of God."[4]

Then they sang a song[5] and went to the Mount of Olives. Jesus told them, "Tonight you'll be threatened because of me. It's written,

> *'I will kill the shepherd and the sheep will scatter.'*
> *"But once I have wakened, I'll go ahead of you into Galilee."*

6 Nine months before the Nazis executed him, theologian Dietrich Bonhoeffer wrote this in a letter to his friend, the theologian Eberhard Bethge:

> It is only by living completely in this world that one learns to have faith. I mean living unreservedly in life's duties, problems, successes and failures, experiences and perplexities. In so doing we throw ourselves completely into the arms of God, taking seriously, not our own suffering, but those of God in the world—watching with Christos in Gethsemane. That, I think, is faith; that is *metanoia*.
>
> —Dietrich Bonhoeffer, *Letters and Papers from Prison* (New York: Macmillan, 1971), 369–370

7 "There is more here than the fear of death; there is the awe of the creature before the *mysterium tremendum*, before the shuddering secret of the number. And the old tales come back into our mind as strangely parallel.... Yahweh who waylaid Moses by night, and of Jacob who wrestled with God 'until the breaking of the day.'"

> —Rudolf Otto, *The Idea of the Holy*, trans. John W. Harvey (New York: Oxford University Press, 1958), 84–85

8 This is a powerful instance of Jesus's spiritual introversion, his constant and intense relationship to the Father. Jungian astrologer Alice O. Howell has examined this tendency in terms of the Piscean Age that corresponds with the era of Christianity:

> One of the trends of the Age of Pisces was the withdrawal of men and women from the world into hermitages and, later, monasteries, in order to meditate, pray, and pursue a mystical and introverted direction. (In the natural zodiac, Pisces is the twelfth sign, and the Twelfth House in any chart rules one's attitude toward seclusion and introspection.)
>
> —Alice O. Howell, *The Heavens Declare: Astrological Ages and the Evolution of Consciousness* (Wheaton, Il: Quest Books, 2006), 227

Peter said, "Everyone else might be afraid, but I won't be."

Jesus said to him, "Listen to me. Today, this very evening, before the rooster crows twice, you'll disown me three times."

Peter spoke more passionately, "I'll die with you before I disown you in any way at all." They all said the same.

Then they came to the place known as Gethsemane. He told his followers, "Sit here while I pray."[6]

He took Peter, James, and John with him and became delirious and distressed. He told them, "My soul is incredibly sad. I feel like death. Stay with me and keep an eye out."[7]

He went ahead a ways and fell to the ground.[8] He prayed that if it were at all possible the moment would pass. He said, "Abba, Father, with you everything is possible. Relieve me of this cup. But I pray that your wish is fulfilled, not mine."

He went back and found his followers sleeping. He said to Peter, Simon, "Are you asleep? Couldn't you stay awake for an hour? Be alert and pray so that you aren't tempted. The spirit is willing, but the flesh is weak."

He went off again to pray and said the same words. He returned and found them asleep once again. Their eyelids were heavy and they couldn't even respond to him.

A third time he came to them and said, "All right. Are you still sleeping? That's over now. The time has come. Look. The son of man will now be betrayed into the hands of those who don't know what they're doing. Get up. Let's go. The betrayer is here."

He hadn't finished speaking when Judas, one of the twelve, arrived from the chief priests and experts in the law with a mob armed with swords and clubs. The betrayer had given them a signal, saying, "I'll kiss the one you want. Take hold of him and rush him away and secure him."

As soon as he arrived, he went directly to Jesus and said, "Master, master" and kissed him. They seized Jesus and took

9   "Jews today find it difficult to appreciate that at the center of the spiritual life
     of their ancestors stood an institution in which animal sacrifices, libations,
     incense offerings, and other priestly actions were thought to have real effi-
     cacy. Judaism today has much less of this sense of what Christosians might
     call a sacrament."
         —George W. E. Nickelsburg and Michael E. Stone, *Early Judaism: Texts and*
         Documents on Faith and Piety, rev. ed. (Minneapolis: Fortress Press, 2009), 2

10   This young man is the focus of much discussion among Gospel scholars, for
     he appears in the extracanonical *Secret Gospel of Mark*. Some think he is Laza-
     rus, and that the linen garment is his burial shroud.
         —Miles Fowler, "Identification of the Bethany Youth in the *Secret Gospel of Mark*
         with other Figures Found in Mark and John," *Journal of Higher Criticism* 5,
         no. 1 (Spring 1998): 3–22

him away. Someone near at hand drew a sword and struck the high priest's servant, cutting off his ear.

Jesus said, "Have you come with swords and clubs to arrest me as though I were a thief? Every day I was with you in the Temple[9] and you didn't take me. But the scriptures have to be fulfilled."

The mob abandoned him and escaped.

There was a young man following him wearing a linen shawl over his naked body. The young man grabbed Jesus and left the linen shawl behind and ran away naked.[10]

They led Jesus to the high priest, who had around him all the chief priests, elders, and experts in the law. Peter followed at a distance and even ventured into the palace of the high priest. He sat with the servants and warmed himself by the fire. The chief priests and the assembly looked for witnesses against Jesus to put him to death, but they couldn't find any. Some lied, but their testimonies conflicted. But some got up and perjured themselves, saying, "We heard him say that he would destroy the Temple that is handmade and build another that is not made by humans." But that testimony conflicted, as well.

The high priest stood up in the middle of everyone and said, "Won't you respond? Is there substance in these accusations?"

Jesus remained silent. The high priest again asked him, "Are you Christos, the son of the Holy One?"

Jesus answered, "I am. You'll see the son of man sitting at the right hand of power, arriving on clouds in the sky."

The high priest ripped his clothes and said, "Do we need any further testimony? You have heard the blasphemy. What is your judgment?"

Everyone judged him guilty and deserving of death.

They spit on him and covered his face and slapped him and said, "Prophesy." Even servants struck him with their hands.

11 The rooster is clearly an image connected to dawn and the rising sun. In Zachariah's chant he describes Christos as "the dawn rising on us." Greek scholar David Fideler, equating Jesus with the Logos, says that the light that "illuminates the inner recesses of the heart with eternal, spiritual knowledge" is the sun of God. In his darkest moment Peter hears the sound of the sun dawning and realizes his failure and his task, to be the sun and not the shadow.
   —David Fideler, *Jesus Christ, Sun of God: Ancient Cosmology and Early Christian Symbolism* (Wheaton, IL: Quest Books, 1993), 51

Peter was down in the palace area when a maid of the high priest approached. She saw Peter warming himself and stared at him. "You were with Jesus of Nazareth."

He denied it, saying, "I don't know what you're saying." He went out to the veranda and a rooster crowed. Another maid saw him and said to those around, "This man was one of them."

Peter denied it again. A little later, someone in the group said to Peter, "I'm sure you're one of them. You're a Galilean. Your accent makes it clear."

Peter cursed and swore. "I don't know what you're talking about."

The rooster crowed a second time and Peter remembered what Jesus had said, "Before the rooster crows twice, you'll disown me three times." Thinking about it, he wept.[11]

1   This accusation of being king of the Jews, later written on a banner on the
    cross, has many implications: People become unhinged when they sense
    treason or lack of patriotism; Jesus's contemporaries could not distinguish
    between social change and political challenge; they did not understand the
    genre of Jesus's teachings—that is, they did not appreciate parable and story
    as serious fictions about how to live. In essence, Jesus's crucifixion reflects a
    mistake in genre.

2   Justice often depends more on passion than reason. People were profoundly
    threatened by Jesus's anti-authoritarian teaching, so they expressed a pref-
    erence for the release of Barabbas, a name that for us suggests "barbarian,"
    rather than the peaceable teaching of Jesus.

3   "The cross is no arbitrary intrusion into the life of Jesus. It is the natural out-
    come of a life of solidarity with the poor and the outcasts and of confronta-
    tion with the powerful who oppress them."
        —George M. Soares-Prabhu, *The Dharma of Jesus*, ed. Francis X. D'Sa
        (Maryknoll, NY: Orbis Books, 2003), 95

Chapter 15

Early morning. The chief priests consult with the elders and clerks and the whole assembly. They tie Jesus up and take him away and give him over to Pilate. Pilate asks him, "Are you the king of the Jews?"[1]

"Is that what you say?" Jesus responds.

The chief priests had made several accusations, so Pilate asked once more, "Aren't you going to respond? Do you know that they're accusing you of many things?"

Jesus remained silent and Pilate was frustrated.

It was the custom at the festival to release a prisoner chosen by the people. In prison was a rebel who had committed murder during an uprising—Barabbas.

A crowd formed and asked Pilate to do what was customary.

"Would you like me to release the king of the Jews?" Pilate asked, knowing that the chief priests had surrendered Jesus to him purely out of envy. But the chief priests had encouraged the crowd to ask for Barabbas to be released instead.[2]

"What will I do with this one, the one you call "king of the Jews"?

"Crucify him."

"Why? What crime has he committed?"

They shouted more loudly, "Crucify him."[3]

So Pilate, hoping to pacify the people, released Barabbas and turned over Jesus to be tortured and crucified.

4 From very early times, devotional literature has focused on this story of Simon carrying the cross. His task is part of the Stations that became a ritual for those meditating on the execution of Jesus. He represents everyone carrying his or her own cross, reflecting the archetypal nature of Jesus's fate and the spiritual poetry in the Gospels.

5 "A Christian poem of the third century begins with the words: There is a place that we believe is the center of the world. The Jews give it the native name Golgotha."
   —Hugo Rahner, *Greek Myths and Christian Mystery* (New York: Biblo and Tannen, 1971), 62

6 "Abelard offered as an explanation for the crucifixion: that the Son of God came down into this world to be crucified to waken our hearts to compassion, and thus to turn our minds from the gross concerns of raw life in the world to the specifically human values of self-giving in shared suffering."
   —Joseph Campbell with Bill Moyers, *The Power of Myth*, ed. Betty Sue Flowers (New York: Doubleday, 1988), 116

7 There was an overshadowing at his conception, and now there is an overshadowing at his death. This is the cosmic Christos. Nature participates in the sad moment of execution. The spiritual realm is never only interior but always reaches out into the world. At times the Father of the Sky brightened that realm with a holy spirit. Now he is absent or hidden.

The guards led Jesus away to the palace, the Praetorium, and called out the whole company of soldiers. They wrapped a purple robe around him and wove a crown of thorns and pressed it on his head. They shouted, "Hail, king of the Jews." They spit on him and hit him on the head with a club and got down on their knees and paid him mock homage. After making fun of him, they took off his purple robe and gave him back his own clothes and led him out for the crucifixion.

A man from Cyrene, Simon, the father of Alexander and Rufus, on his way in from the countryside, happened to be passing by. They compelled him to carry the cross.⁴ They led Jesus to the place known as Golgotha,⁵ the Place of the Skull, and gave him wine mixed with myrrh, but he didn't accept it. They crucified him and then divided his clothes and tossed dice to decide who would get what.

They crucified him at nine in the morning. The charge against him read: "King of the Jews." They crucified two thieves with him, one on his left and one on his right. Passersby shook their heads. "Bah! You'd destroy the Temple and rebuild it in three days. Come down from that cross. Rescue yourself." The chief priests and clerks also mocked him: "He saved others but he can't save himself. The man of oil, the king of Israel, should come down from that cross now so we can see and believe." The ones crucified with him also taunted him.⁶

At noon darkness fell over the whole area until three in the afternoon.⁷ At three o'clock Jesus sobbed loudly, "*Eloi, Eloi, lema sabachthani?*—My God, my God, why have you abandoned me?" Bystanders heard this and said, "He's calling on Elijah. Listen." Someone ran and soaked a sponge in sour wine and stuck it on a stick and offered it to him and said, "Let's see if Elijah will come and take him down." Then Jesus cried out loudly and breathed his last breath. The Temple curtain split in two from top to bottom. A centurion was standing in front of Jesus and

8 History turned the childlike, androgynous teaching of Jesus into a patriarchal and hierarchical structure of required beliefs and rules. But the Book of Mark shows the supreme moment of crucifixion, with all its echoes of Eden, the Tree of Life, and the center of the world, a tableau largely composed of women. This detail is not just about history and fact but also about the substance of the teaching: It has a strong feminine context and foundation.

saw how he breathed his last breath and said, "This was indeed the son of God."

Women were watching from a distance, among them Mary Magdalene and Mary the mother of James the younger and of Joses, and Salome. When he had stayed in Galilee, they had followed him and had taken care of him. Several other women had come to Jerusalem with him.[8]

It was evening of the Day of Preparation, the day before the Sabbath. A respected advisor, Joseph of Arimathaea, who was waiting for the kingdom of God, appeared and went boldly to Pilate and asked for Jesus's body.

Pilate was shocked to hear that Jesus was already dead. He called for the centurion and checked to be sure that Jesus had died. The centurion assured him of the fact and Pilate let Joseph have the body. Joseph bought some linen and took the body down and wrapped it in the linen and put it in a tomb cut from rock. He rolled a stone against the entrance. Mary Magdalene and Mary the mother of Joses saw where he was placed.

1   Another word of amazement, this one with the connotation of terror. Why
    be alarmed at the young man in white? This scene is characteristic of Mark's
    imagination. He leaves us with mysteries and invites us to be amazed and
    disturbed by all that is happening.

2   "To rise from history to mystery is to experience the resurrection of the body
    here now as an eternal reality; to experience the *parousia*, the presence in the
    present, which is the spirit; to experience the reincarnation of the incarna-
    tion, the second coming; which is coming in us."
        —Norman O. Brown, *Love's Body* (New York: Vintage Books, 1966), 214

    Egeiro is the key word in the Gospels for waking up, getting up, and resur-
    recting. It is the word used when, in the Book of Matthew, Jesus instructs his
    students to "wake up the unconscious." It is the word used in the first chapter
    of the Book of Mark when Jesus lifts up Peter's mother-in-law by the hand
    from her bed.

3   "The message is not sent. The message does not arrive. In its place—t-error....
    The gospel according to Mark 'ends' with the silence of three women. 'They
    say nothing....' In the wake of death, there is nothing left to say. Always
    nothing left to say. But how to say it? To say it again? And again, and again?
    Without end?"
        —Mark C. Taylor, in Robert P. Scharlemann, ed., "Unending Strokes" *Theology
        at the End of the Century: A Dialogue of the Postmodern* (Charlottesville: University
        Press of Virginia, 1990), 147

Chapter 16

The Sabbath was over, and Mary Magdalene, Mary the mother of James, and Salome bought spices to anoint Jesus's body. Early on the first day of the week, just after sunrise, they returned to the tomb and wondered who might roll the stone away from the tomb's entrance. But they looked and saw that the huge stone had already been moved. Entering the tomb they saw a young man dressed in a white robe sitting on the right side and were alarmed.[1]

"Don't be shocked," he said. "You're looking for Jesus of Nazareth, who was crucified. He got up[2] and is not here. Look, this is where they laid him. Go tell Peter and the others that he has gone ahead of you to Galilee. You'll see him there, as he said you would."

Shaken and confused, the women left and hurried away from the tomb. They didn't say a word to anyone, they were so afraid.[3]

Acknowledgments

Translating and commenting on *The Book of Mark* brought up many fresh questions and challenges. I found the process exciting, and along the way I had help from many people. I would like to thank my old friends and neighbors Carol Renwick and Hugh Renwick for helpful conversations on the meaning of the stories. George W. E. Nickelsburg, a distinguished scholar and imaginative man, gave me constant encouragement and many useful ideas and corrections. Pat Toomay, whose skill on the football field transferred with incredible power to studies in cultural meaning, offered subtle shifts in direction. At home, Abe and Ajeet supported the project, especially at times when I doubted its relevance. Hari Kirin Khalsa constantly feeds my mind and imagination and helped me steer my course through this fresh territory. As before, I have to say that I am lucky to have an editors like Emily Wichland and Jon O'Neal and a publicist like Leah Brewer. They are skilled and strong in their vision and yet they can also let me experiment. More indirectly, perhaps, I feel the inspiration of my old professor John Dominic Crossan, and of the writings of Robert Funk, Marcus Borg, and George Aichele.

Notes

Introduction to Gospel

1. Translations and writings on the Gospels often include chapter and verse when passages are cited. I do not include the verse because I want the reader to have a fresh, clear experience of the text. I hope that the absence of verse numbers will intensify the feeling of reading poetry, rather than prose While this may make it slightly more difficult to navigate the text, I think the emphasis on the poetic is more important.

2. John G. Neihardt, *Black Elk Speaks* (New York: Pocket Books, 1959), 25.

Introduction to the Book of Mark

1. Ralph Waldo Emerson, "Divinity School Address," delivered before the senior class in Divinity College, Cambridge, MA. July 15, 1838, www.emersoncentral.com /divaddr.htm.

Suggestions for Further Reading

Aichele, George. *Jesus Framed*. London: Routledge, 1996.

Borg, Marcus. *Conversations with Scripture: The Gospel of Mark*. Harrisburg, NY: Morehouse Publishing, 2009.

Cotter, Wendy J. *The Christ of the Miracle Stories: Portrait through Encounter*. Grand Rapids, MI: Baker Academic, 2010.

Crossan, John Dominic. *The Essential Jesus*. San Francisco: HarperSanFrancisco, 1989.

———. *Jesus: A Revolutionary Biography*. San Francisco: HarperSanFrancisco, 1994.

Funk, Robert W., and the Jesus Seminar. *The Acts of Jesus: The Search for the Authentic Deeds of Jesus*. San Francisco: HarperSanFrancisco, 1998.

Moore, Thomas. *Writing in the Sand: Jesus and the Soul of the Gospels*. Carlsbad, CA: Hay House, 2009.

Moore, Thomas. *Care of the Soul*. New York: HarperCollins, 1992.

———. *Gospel—The Book of Matthew: A New Translation with Commentary—Jesus Spirituality for Everyone*. Woodstock, VT: SkyLight Paths, 2016.

About the Author

Thomas Moore is the author of the best-selling book *Care of the Soul* and many other books on deepening spirituality and cultivating soul in every aspect of life. He has been a monk, a musician, a university professor, and a psychotherapist, and today he lectures widely on holistic medicine, spirituality, psychotherapy, and the arts. He lectures frequently in Ireland and has a special love of Irish culture.

He has a PhD in religion from Syracuse University and has won several awards for his work, including an honorary doctorate from Lesley University and the Humanitarian Award from Einstein Medical School of Yeshiva University. Three of his books have won the prestigious Books for a Better Life awards. He writes fiction and music and often works with his wife, Hari Kirin, who is an artist and yoga instructor. He writes regular columns for *Spirituality & Health, Patheos. Com* and the *Huffington Post*. For more about him, visit thomasmooresoul.com.

Thomas Moore is available to speak to your group or at your event. For more information, please contact us at www.thomasmooresoul.com